THE
MOHAWK

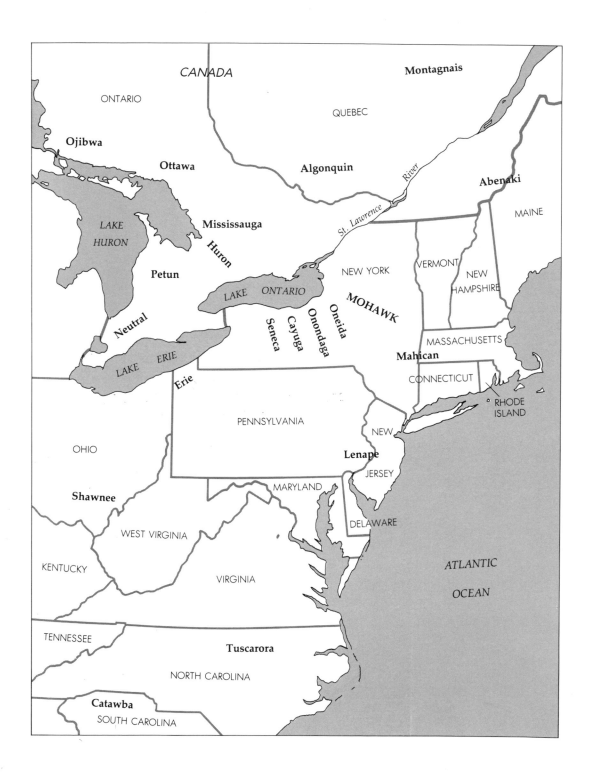

THE
MOHAWK

Nancy Bonvillain
New School for Social Research

Frank W. Porter III
General Editor

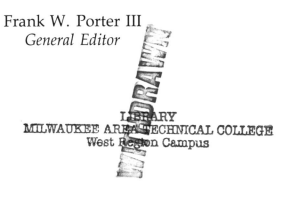

CHELSEA HOUSE PUBLISHERS
New York   Philadelphia

On the cover   A pair of dyed deerskin moccasins decorated with quillwork, made by Mohawk artisans in the late 19th or early 20th century.

Chelsea House Publishers
Editor-in-Chief   Remmel Nunn
Managing Editor   Karyn Gullen Browne
Copy Chief   Mark Rifkin
Picture Editor   Adrian G. Allen
Art Director   Maria Epes
Assistant Art Director   Noreen Romano
Manufacturing Manager   Gerald Levine
Systems Manager   Lindsey Ottman
Production Manager   Joseph Romano
Production Coordinator   Marie Claire Cebrián

Indians of North America
Senior Editor   Liz Sonneborn

Staff for **THE MOHAWK**
Copy Editor   Laurie Kahn
Editorial Assistant   Michele Haddad
Designer   Debora Smith
Picture Researcher   Sandy Jones

3 5 7 9 8 6 4 2

Library of Congress Cataloging-in-Publication Data

Bonvillain, Nancy
    The Mohawk/by Nancy Bonvillain.
        p.   cm.—(Indians of North America)
    Includes bibliographical references and index.
    Summary: Examines the history, culture, and traditions of the Mohawk Indians.
    ISBN 0-7910-1636-6
        0-7910-1679-X
    1. Mohawk Indians. [1. Mohawk Indians. 2. Indians of North America.] I. Title II. Series: Indians of North America (Chelsea House Publishers)
                                                            91-9831
E99.M8B66 1991   CIP
973'.04975—dc20   AC

CONTENTS

INDIANS OF NORTH AMERICA

CHELSEA HOUSE PUBLISHERS

INDIANS OF NORTH AMERICA: CONFLICT AND SURVIVAL

Frank W. Porter III

> *The Indians survived our open intention of wiping them out, and since the tide turned they have even weathered our good intentions toward them, which can be much more deadly.*
>
> John Steinbeck
> *America and Americans*

When Europeans first reached the North American continent, they found hundreds of tribes occupying a vast and rich country. The newcomers quickly recognized the wealth of natural resources. They were not, however, so quick or willing to recognize the spiritual, cultural, and intellectual riches of the people they called Indians.

The Indians of North America examines the problems that develop when people with different cultures come together. For American Indians, the consequences of their interaction with non-Indian people have been both productive and tragic. The Europeans believed they had "discovered" a "New World," but their religious bigotry, cultural bias, and materialistic world view kept them from appreciating and understanding the people who lived in it. All too often they attempted to change the way of life of the indigenous people. The Spanish conquistadores wanted the Indians as a source of labor. The Christian missionaries, many of whom were English, viewed them as potential converts. French traders and trappers used the Indians as a means to obtain pelts. As Francis Parkman, the 19th-century historian, stated, "Spanish civilization crushed the Indian; English civilization scorned and neglected him; French civilization embraced and cherished him."

Nearly 500 years later, many people think of American Indians as curious vestiges of a distant past, waging a futile war to survive in a Space Age society. Even today, our understanding of the history and culture of American Indians is too often derived from unsympathetic, culturally biased, and inaccurate reports. The American Indian, described and portrayed in thousands of movies, television programs, books, articles, and government studies, has either been raised to the status of the "noble savage" or disparaged as the "wild Indian" who resisted the westward expansion of the American frontier.

Where in this popular view are the real Indians, the human beings and communities whose ancestors can be traced back to ice-age hunters? Where are the creative and indomitable people whose sophisticated technologies used the natural resources to ensure their survival, whose military skill might even have prevented European settlement of North America if not for devastating epidemics and disruption of the ecology? Where are the men and women who are today diligently struggling to assert their legal rights and express once again the value of their heritage?

The various Indian tribes of North America, like people everywhere, have a history that includes population expansion, adaptation to a range of regional environments, trade across wide networks, internal strife, and warfare. This was the reality. Europeans justified their conquests, however, by creating a mythical image of the New World and its native people. In this myth, the New World was a virgin land, waiting for the Europeans. The arrival of Christopher Columbus ended a timeless primitiveness for the original inhabitants.

Also part of this myth was the debate over the origins of the American Indians. Fantastic and diverse answers were proposed by the early explorers, missionairies, and settlers. Some thought that the Indians were descended from the Ten Lost Tribes of Israel, others that they were descended from inhabitants of the lost continent of Atlantis. One writer suggested that the Indians had reached North America in another Noah's ark.

A later myth, perpetrated by many historians, focused on the relentless persecution during the past five centuries until only a scattering of these "primitive" people remained to be herded onto reservations. This view fails to chronicle the overt and covert ways in which the Indians successfully coped with the intruders.

All of these myths presented one-sided interpretations that ignored the complexity of European and American events and policies. All left serious questions unanswered. What were the origins of the American Indians? Where did they come from? How and when did they get to the New World? What was their life—their culture—really like?

In the late 1800s, anthropologists and archaeologists in the Smithsonian Institution's newly created Bureau of American Ethnology in Washington,

D.C., began to study scientifically the history and culture of the Indians of North America. They were motivated by an honest belief that the Indians were on the verge of extinction and that along with them would vanish their languages, religious beliefs, technology, myths, and legends. These men and women went out to visit, study, and record data from as many Indian communities as possible before this information was forever lost.

By this time there was a new myth in the national consciousness. American Indians existed as figures in the American past. They had performed a historical mission. They had challenged white settlers who trekked across the continent. Once conquered, however, they were supposed to accept graciously the way of life of their conquerors.

The reality again was different. American Indians resisted both actively and passively. They refused to lose their unique identity, to be assimilated into white society. Many whites viewed the Indians not only as members of a conquered nation but also as "inferior" and "unequal." The rights of the Indians could be expanded, contracted, or modified as the conquerors saw fit. In every generation, white society asked itself what to do with the American Indians. Their answers have resulted in the twists and turns of federal Indian policy.

There were two general approaches. One way was to raise the Indians to a "higher level" by "civilizing" them. Zealous missionaries considered it their Christian duty to elevate the Indian through conversion and scanty education. The other approach was to ignore the Indians until they disappeared under pressure from the ever-expanding white society. The myth of the "vanishing Indian" gave stronger support to the latter option, helping to justify the taking of the Indians' land.

Prior to the end of the 18th century, there was no national policy on Indians simply because the American nation had not yet come into existence. American Indians similarly did not possess a political or social unity with which to confront the various Europeans. They were not homogeneous. Rather, they were loosely formed bands and tribes, speaking nearly 300 languages and thousands of dialects. The collective identity felt by Indians today is a result of their common experiences of defeat and/or mistreatment at the hands of whites.

During the colonial period, the British crown did not have a coordinated policy toward the Indians of North America. Specific tribes (most notably the Iroquois and the Cherokee) became military and political pawns used by both the crown and the individual colonies. The success of the American Revolution brought no immediate change. When the United States acquired new territory from France and Mexico in the early 19th century, the federal government wanted to open this land to settlement by homesteaders. But the Indian tribes that lived on this land had signed treaties with European governments assuring their title to the land. Now the United States assumed legal responsibility for honoring these treaties.

At first, President Thomas Jefferson believed that the Louisiana Purchase contained sufficient land for both the Indians and the white population. Within a generation, though, it became clear that the Indians would not be allowed to remain. In the 1830s the federal government began to coerce the eastern tribes to sign treaties agreeing to relinquish their ancestral land and move west of the Mississippi River. Whenever these negotiations failed, President Andrew Jackson used the military to remove the Indians. The southeastern tribes, promised food and transportation during their removal to the West, were instead forced to walk the "Trail of Tears." More than 4,000 men, woman, and children died during this forced march. The "removal policy" was successful in opening the land to homesteaders, but it created enormous hardships for the Indians.

By 1871 most of the tribes in the United States had signed treaties ceding most or all of their ancestral land in exchange for reservations and welfare. The treaty terms were intended to bind both parties for all time. But in the General Allotment Act of 1887, the federal government changed its policy again. Now the goal was to make tribal members into individual landowners and farmers, encouraging their absorption into white society. This policy was advantageous to whites who were eager to acquire Indian land, but it proved disastrous for the Indians. One hundred thirty-eight million acres of reservation land were subdivided into tracts of 160, 80, or as little as 40 acres, and allotted tribe members on an individual basis. Land owned in this way was said to have "trust status" and could not be sold. But the surplus land—all Indian land not allotted to individuals—was opened (for sale) to white settlers. Ultimately, more than 90 million acres of land were taken from the Indians by legal and illegal means.

The resulting loss of land was a catastrophe for the Indians. It was necessary to make it illegal for Indians to sell their land to non-Indians. The Indian Reorganization Act of 1934 officially ended the allotment period. Tribes that voted to accept the provisions of this act were reorganized, and an effort was made to purchase land within preexisting reservations to restore an adequate land base.

Ten years later, in 1944, federal Indian policy again shifted. Now the federal government wanted to get out of the "Indian business." In 1953 an act of Congress named specific tribes whose trust status was to be ended "at the earliest possible time." This new law enabled the United States to end unilaterally, whether the Indians wished it or not, the special status that protected the land in Indian tribal reservations. In the 1950s federal Indian policy was to transfer federal responsibility and jurisdiction to state governments, encourage the physical relocation of Indian peoples from reservations to urban areas, and hasten the termination, or extinction, of tribes.

Between 1954 and 1962 Congress passed specific laws authorizing the termination of more than 100 tribal groups. The stated purpose of the termination policy was to ensure the full and complete integration of Indians into American society. However, there is a less benign way to interpret this legislation. Even as termination was being discussed in Congress, 133 separate bills were introduced to permit the transfer of trust land ownership from Indians to non-Indians.

With the Johnson administration in the 1960s the federal government began to reject termination. In the 1970s yet another Indian policy emerged. Known as "self-determination," it favored keeping the protective role of the federal government while increasing tribal participation in, and control of, important areas of local government. In 1983 President Reagan, in a policy statement on Indian affairs, restated the unique "government is government" relationship of the United States with the Indians. However, federal programs since then have moved toward transferring Indian affairs to individual states, which have long desired to gain control of Indian land and resources.

As long as American Indians retain power, land, and resources that are coveted by the states and the federal government, there will continue to be a "clash of cultures," and the issues will be contested in the courts, Congress, the White House, and even in the international human rights community. To give all Americans a greater comprehension of the issues and conflicts involving American Indians today is a major goal of this series. These issues are not easily understood, nor can these conflicts be readily resolved. The study of North American Indian history and culture is a necessary and important step toward that comprehension. All Americans must learn the history of the relations between the Indians and the federal government, recognize the unique legal status of the Indians, and understand the heritage and cultures of the Indians of North America.

A 1664 French engraving of Iroquois territory. Early European explorers were stunned by the rich environment they found in North America.

ANCESTORS

In 1644, a Dutch minister named Johannes Megapolensis visited Mohawk territory and made the following observations:

The land is good, and fruitful in everything which supplies human needs. The country is very mountainous, partly soil, partly rocks, and with elevations so exceeding high that they appear to almost touch the clouds. Thereon grow the finest fir trees the eye ever saw. There are also in this country oaks, alders, beeches, elms, willows, etc. In the forests, and here and there along the water side, and on the islands, there grows an abundance of chestnuts, plums, hazel nuts, large walnuts of several sorts. The ground on the hills is covered with bushes of blueberries; the ground in the flat land near the rivers is covered with strawberries, which grow here so plentifully in the fields, that one can lie down and eat them.

Grapevines also grow here naturally in great abundance along the roads, paths and creeks. I have seen whole pieces of land where vine stood by vine and grew very luxuriantly, climbing to the top of the largest and loftiest trees. In the forests is great plenty of deer. There are also many partridges, heath-hens and pigeons that fly together in thousands, and a great number of all kinds of fowl, swans, geese, ducks which sport upon the river in thousands. Beside the deer and elks, there are panthers, bears, wolves, and foxes. In the river is a great plenty of all kinds of fish—pike, eels, perch, lampreys, cat fish, sun fish, shad, bass, and sturgeon.

In this bountiful environment lived the Mohawk. This powerful nation once decided the fortunes of many peoples—Indian and non-Indian alike —in what is now the United States and Canada.

The Mohawk whom Megapolensis visited in the 17th century were descendants of peoples who in ancient times had lived in present-day New York State. Beginning about 10,000 years ago, northeastern North America was inhabited by men and women who subsisted by hunting animals and gathering wild plants, fruits, and nuts. Gradually, over many thousands of years, they developed sophisticated tools and utensils and refined such arts as pottery making and basketry.

In order to survive, these prehistoric people had to move frequently, following the animals they hunted and searching out new sources of wild plants and fruits. They dealt with the hardships they encountered by living in small groups and offering each other assistance and companionship.

It is impossible to fix exact dates for the arrival of ancestors of the modern Mohawk in the Northeast, but they probably migrated from areas to the west sometime between 1700 B.C. and 1200 B.C. After that time, three major periods of cultural development occurred in the Northeast—the Early Woodland period, the Middle Woodland period, and the Late Woodland period. These stages can be identified by continuities or changes in people's foods, housing, methods of making tools and utensils, and styles of decorating pottery and other equipment.

One of the first types of societies (or traditions) associated with the ancestors of the Mohawk is called Meadowood. This tradition existed around

1000 B.C., during the Early Woodland phase in central New York State. Although people in those times were nomadic, following their animal prey, they maintained a central base area where they lived between hunting and fishing expeditions.

Objects have been found at Meadowood sites that were not of local origin. Among these items were conch shells from the Gulf of Mexico, copper from Lake Superior, silver from Ontario, mica (a mineral) from the southern Appalachian Mountains, and grizzly-bear teeth from the Rocky Mountains. These finds indicate that prehistoric peoples had long-distance trading networks through which they exchanged local goods for valuables from regions thousands of miles away. The existence of trade items also proves that people did not live in total isolation from one another but established friendly contacts with their neighbors.

Cultures like those of Meadowood continued for hundreds of years. Then in the Middle Woodland period, significant changes in the Indians' way of life took place. By around A.D. 200, settlement patterns had changed. People constructed larger villages that were relocated every few years, apparently to bring them closer to food sources. The people's houses, made of bark and earth, could be rebuilt in a relatively short time. They were spacious enough to accommodate several families.

Middle Woodland villages were located near rivers, giving residents easy access to travel routes. The typical

A model of an Iroquoian village of 11 longhouses surrounded by a palisade.

mode of transportation was by canoe in rivers and lakes, for traveling on foot through the region's dense forests was slow and difficult.

Middle Woodland peoples relied on a great variety of wild foods, including animals such as deer and bear, many species of fish, and different kinds of nuts, berries, and plants. Through trade they were able to acquire goods, including smoking pipes manufactured from stone originating in other parts of North America and pendants made from stone and shark's teeth. These people also possessed copper and shell beads that they presumably used to decorate clothing and other objects.

A typical Middle Woodland village, settled in about A.D. 800 to 900, was Hunter's Home, situated on the Mo-

hawk River near present-day Schenectady. People at Hunter's Home had begun to grow some of their own food. Even though seeds or crops have not been found, the discovery at the site of mortars and pestles—utensils used for grinding seeds and corn kernels—indicates that people there must have grown corn.

Over time, the Indians of the Northeast came to rely more and more on farming for their food supply. The people of Central America, who had learned to cultivate crops long before, probably contributed indirectly to the Woodland Indians' knowledge of farming techniques. Just as Woodland peoples traded for raw materials, utensils, and beads, they also exchanged ideas. Over hundreds of years, the innovations of one Indian group could be transmitted to peoples thousands of miles away.

Farming was advantageous because it gave people a secure source of food. But Middle Woodland people did not abandon their old ways completely. They continued to gather wild plants, fruits, and nuts and to fish and hunt in the forests. A greater variety and abundance of food led to larger and more permanent villages. Middle Woodland peoples began to alter their settlement patterns in different seasons. During the spring and summer, when foods were plentiful, they lived in large villages. They split up into smaller groups after harvests in autumn and winter, when plants and animals became scarce.

The Late Woodland period began in about A.D. 1000. A major cultural phase of this period was the Owasco tradition, which lasted from A.D. 1000 to 1300. Many cultural changes were adopted during this time.

In the Owasco phase, people shifted their villages from river sites to hilltops. Although no one knows for certain why this was done, Owasco peoples probably sought safety on hills from their enemies. In addition to protection given by hilltop locations, people surrounded their villages with palisades—walls of long poles spaced a few feet apart that made it difficult for intruders to enter their villages undetected. Some settlements were protected further by ditches dug outside the palisades and by

Late Iroquoian artifacts: (a, b) pottery fragments; (c) stone pipe bowl; (d) deer antler harpoon; (e) stone scraper; (f) needle used to sew nets; (g) stone tortoise amulet; (h) stone and bone arrowheads; (i) pottery pipes; (j) dagger made from a human bone.

earthen barricades built inside. Villagers would probably have created such elaborate structures only if they were afraid of being attacked. Although it is unknown who their enemies were or what caused the warfare, they may have fought with neighboring peoples for control of valuable farmland.

Owasco villages became larger and more concentrated. The small, dispersed settlements of earlier times were abandoned because it was easier to protect a few concentrated areas than numerous isolated locales. Oblong houses covered with elm bark were typical Owasco dwellings. Several families lived in each house. They subsisted on the crops they grew, supplemented by wild plants and animals. Corn was their most important crop. Several varieties of beans and squash were also produced.

The final cultural phase within the Late Woodland period began around A.D. 1300 and is called the Iroquoian tradition. The term *Iroquoian* is used to describe a group of peoples who spoke related languages and had similar economic systems, social customs, and religious beliefs. The Iroquoians emerged from earlier Owasco societies, retaining the same basic way of life but developing and elaborating certain elements of their culture.

Early Iroquoian villages have been excavated near present-day Albany, Kingston, and New Paltz in New York State. These villages were relatively permanent and were relocated every 10 or 20 years to a distance of perhaps 2 or 3 miles. Trails, some of which still exist, connected villages to frequently used hunting and fishing stations. Meat and fish were supplemented by crops, including corn, beans, squash, melons, and sunflowers.

Iroquoian residences were large, rectangular structures made of wooden poles covered with elm bark. These longhouses had doors located at each end. Inside there was a central row of hearths for cooking and heating. A hearth was shared by two families, each having separate living quarters. Longhouses usually accommodated as many as 10 families.

Iroquoian peoples built ever thicker and sturdier palisades around their villages, which suggests that warfare increased. They often erected two or three rows of poles rather than the single rows that had been built in earlier times. As settlements became more concentrated and as warfare increased, long-distance trade diminished. Few materials originating in faraway places have been found at Iroquoian sites, suggesting that individual groups had become more self-sufficient.

Geographic separation eventually led distinct groups to form among the Iroquoians. They soon became divided into several nations, each with its own name. One such nation was the Kanienkehaka (ga-nyen-ge-HA-ga), meaning "people of the place of flint." These people, known to non-Indians as the Mohawk, would play a dramatic role in the history of North America. ▲

Two Iroquois men carving a wood mask, or false face, in 1909. The man at the left is burning tobacco in order to transfer the spiritual power of the tree to the false face.

PEOPLE
OF THE
PLACE OF FLINT

For centuries, the Kanienkehaka, or the Mohawk, lived in the Mohawk River valley west of what is now the city of Albany in New York State. Their hunting territories extended northward into the Adirondack Mountains and southward along the Susquehanna River to the present-day town of Oneonta. To the west were other Iroquoian nations, including the Oneida, the Onondaga, the Cayuga, and the Seneca. They spoke closely related languages and developed very similar cultures. East of the Mohawk were peoples such as the Mahican, the Housatonic, and the Wappinger. Linked by similar languages and cultures, these groups are known as Algonkians. The ways of life of the Iroquoians and the Algonkians were quite different—a situation that sometimes led to conflicts between the two groups.

At the beginning of their recorded history (approximately A.D. 1500), the Mohawk continued the traditions developed by their Iroquoian ancestors. The Mohawk people lived in three large villages, all located on the south side of the Mohawk River in the heart of the nation's territory. One village, named Tionontoguen (de-yo-non-DO-gen), meaning "valley" or "between two mountains," was referred to as the center or capital. These 3 villages, as well as several smaller ones, were relocated from time to time, probably every 10 or 20 years, when the nutrients in nearby soil had been exhausted and were therefore useless for farming.

The Mohawk lived in large longhouses made of wooden poles covered with earth and elm bark. These longhouses were usually about 25 feet wide and averaged 80 feet in length, although some were as long as 200 feet. A house typically contained a central row of four or five hearths, each accommodating two families of perhaps five or six people. Platforms built along the inner walls, about one foot from the ground, were covered with reed mats or animal pelts and used for seating during the day and sleeping at night. People stored utensils, tools, and food on shelves along the wall. Large bins made of bark were placed between each family's quarters within the longhouse. These bins were used to store corn, dried fruit, and cured deer meat. At the ends of houses, people kept firewood, which they used for both cooking and heating.

Villages were located on hilltops close to the lakes and rivers that provided the major routes of travel. The Mohawk selected their sites near drinking water as well. Small villages contained about 30 longhouses, but larger ones held as many as 100. The people built wooden palisades around their villages for protection against enemy attacks. Planting fields lay outside the boundaries of residential settlements.

Women provided their families with foods from farming. They planted seeds in the spring, weeded fields throughout the summer, and harvested crops in the fall. They used wooden hoes to dig holes for seeds, which they planted in small mounds of earth. Women prepared seeds before planting by soaking them in medicinal solutions for several days. They believed that this procedure kept crows away from their crops. They

planted many varieties of corn and had numerous recipes for its preparation. Corn kernels were typically dried in the sun and baked into breads. Women also prepared corn soups, often adding berries, meat, or fish for flavor.

The relationship between women and food production is symbolized by the belief that a female deity in the ancient past gave corn, beans, and squash to the people. These primary crops are referred to as either the Three Sisters or Our Life Supporters.

Because women performed the farm work, they were considered the owners of their family's fields and produce. Females controlled the distribution of all food within their households. Prominent women also dictated what land could be used by each member of their family.

Women gathered fruits, nuts, and wild potatoes. Strawberries and blueberries were spread in bark trays and dried in the sun for later use. The Mohawk diet also included hickory nuts, walnuts, acorns, and sunflower seeds. Oils from nuts and seeds were used in cooking. In the early spring, women extracted sap from maple trees, which they used to sweeten tea and dishes made from corn.

Men made important contributions to their families' sustenance, providing fish, wild fowl, and animal meat. They hunted deer, elk, moose, bear, beaver, partridge, and wild turkey. Bows and arrows were the basic hunting gear, although men also used wooden traps to capture deer and spears and nets to

A 17th-century engraving of Mohawk women preparing food. Because women performed all the farm work, they were considered to be the owners of their family's crops.

catch birds and fish. Sometimes men and women organized communal deer hunts, during which they could catch as many as 100 animals. During such hunts, the party walked through the woods in two lines forming a V. The hunters shook rattles and made noises to frighten deer and lead them into the narrow space between the two lines. Once trapped inside the V's point, the animals could be easily killed.

In addition to the variety of foods, the Mohawk brewed several types of tea. Some were made from hemlock boughs boiled in water and flavored with maple syrup. Others were brewed from wild spices or sassafras root. Teas were also made from numerous herbs and roots that were known to have medicinal value. Herbal teas were part of the treatment for various ailments. In fact, the people had a great deal of medical knowledge. They learned the healing properties of many plants, tree barks, and oils from fish, snakes, and other animals.

Mohawk women made clothing from deerskin, which they dyed black. In rainy or cold weather, people covered themselves with extra pelts. Footwear consisted of moccasins in most seasons, although in the summer the Mohawk wore slippers made from twined cornhusks. They also donned armbands, wristbands, and deerskin belts, which were often decorated with embroidery. Warriors tattooed their body (especially their chest and shoulders) and face. They favored geometric designs and representations of animals.

Strings or belts of wampum had great ritual value to the Mohawk. Wampum was made from clam shells and was obtained through trade with Indians on Long Island and in coastal New Jersey. The shells were cut into pieces and made into small beads that were strung together or woven into belts. Different patterns formed by the white and purple beads conveyed different messages. Wampum was given to participants on many special occasions, such as funerals. It was also used to commemorate important events, such as visits by prominent guests and the conclusion of treaties with other nations. An account of a specific event was "talked into the wampum" and thereby preserved forever.

The Mohawk enjoyed a variety of games, which were often accompanied by betting on individual contestants or teams. One such sport was a ball game, played by two teams of six or eight men. The object of the game was to carry a small deerskin ball through one of two gates erected at either end of a playing field. The players moved the ball using long sticks with a small net at one end. Participants attempted to intercept

members of the opposite team in order to make them drop the ball or block them from catching it. Before a game started, players decided how many successful goals—generally five to eight—would constitute a victory. This ancient Iroquoian game was a precursor of the modern game of lacrosse.

During winter months, people enjoyed a game called snow snakes. A snow snake was a pole, perhaps five to seven feet long, made of polished hickory wood. It measured approximately one inch wide at its head and gradually narrowed to half that width at the bottom. A snow snake was thrown so that it slid very fast along packed snow. The object of the game was to make the snow snake travel the farthest distance.

The lives of the Mohawk were organized around a yearly cycle of activities, based on the phases of the moon. The pivotal division of a year was called Midwinter. It occurred five nights following the appearance of a new moon after the winter solstice (about December 22). The first economic activity took place two moons after Midwinter, when women went into the woods to obtain sap from maple trees. Next, the men went out to hunt the birds that arrived every spring from the south. The men also caught fish, which filled rivers and lakes in enormous numbers.

Next, women began their farming activities. These tasks occupied the summer and fall, ending with annual harvests. In autumn, men left their villages on hunting expeditions. They returned home by the time of winter

Iroquois men playing snow snakes, drawn by Seneca artist Jesse Cornplanter in 1903. The object of this traditional game was to slide a hickory wood pole across a patch of ice as far as possible.

solstice, and everyone prepared again for Midwinter and a renewal of the yearly cycle.

Mohawk families were related on the basis of descent through women. This kinship system, called matrilineal (from *matri* meaning "mother" and *lineal* meaning "line" or "descent"), linked generations from mother to daughter. The whole society was divided into three clans. A clan is a group of people who consider themselves related and often share stories or myths about their common ancestry. Mohawk clans were named after animals—the bear, the wolf, and the turtle. A person automatically belonged to her or his mother's clan. Since social rules dictated that two people of the same clan could not marry each other, the clan system linked kinship groups to others through marriage.

Clans controlled and distributed farmland to their members. They also owned the longhouses that were inhabited by families related through clan membership. Typically, a household was headed by an elder woman and included her daughters, and the younger women's husbands and children. Sons resided with their mothers until they married. They then moved into their wives' houses.

Marriages were marked with a simple ceremony. Accompanied by her mother and some female relatives and friends, the bride-to-be traveled to the house of her intended husband. When she arrived, she gave a present of corn bread to her future mother-in-law, who returned the honor with a gift of deer meat. Afterward, all in attendance shared in a feast.

The exchange of foods had symbolic meaning. A woman's family offered corn, which was associated with female labor. A man's family reciprocated with deer meat, associated with male labor. Together these gifts represented the interdependence of women and men in the economic well-being of families.

A marriage ideally lasted until the death of one spouse. But if a wife and husband became unhappy with one another, they were free to divorce and seek new mates. However, the couple's mothers frequently tried to mediate disputes and reach a reconciliation.

Women were often referred to as "mothers of the nation," in recognition of the value of their role in the continuity of generations. Another symbolic expression of this occurred in cases of murder. According to Mohawk custom, a murderer's family had to present strings or belts of wampum to the victim's family to atone for the crime. Fines were set at 20 belts for a woman's death and 10 for a man's. The double value of a woman's life was deemed appropriate because it reflected not only the loss of her own life but also the lives of the children she might have borne.

The Mohawk Nation was divided into two sections, or moieties. A moiety (from the French word for half) is a grouping of clans. The Wolf and Turtle clans formed one moiety, the Bear clan

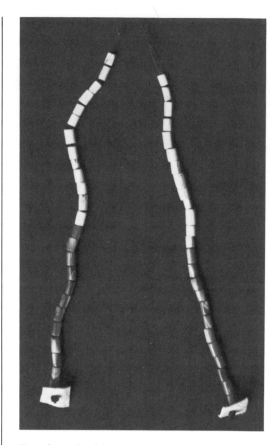

Purple and white beads known as wampum were highly prized by the Mohawk.

constituted the other. Moieties served certain ceremonial functions, one of which was to prepare and conduct funerals for members of the other group. For instance, when a person belonging to the Wolf clan died, Bear clan people arranged the deceased's funeral ceremony. This custom arose because the Mohawk believed that members of the deceased's clan or moiety were too overcome by grief to be able to conduct a proper rite.

THE WAMPUM BIRD

White and purple beads called wampum played an important role in traditional Mohawk society. Weaving these beads into belts, the Mohawk formed colorful patterns that functioned to record and commemorate special events. Wampum belts were often presented as gifts to cement alliances with other peoples.

In his 1976 book, Tales of the Iroquois, *a Mohawk Indian named Tehanetorens recorded the following legend about wampum's meaning to his tribe.*

Long ago, a war party of Mohawks captured a young man of the Wampanoag Nation. For some years, the Mohawks had been at war with these people. The captive boy was allowed to live, and was given permission to move freely about the Mohawk Village. He was closely watched so that he might not escape back to the Wampanoag Country.

One day, a young Mohawk hunter came running into the village. He was filled with excitement, for he had seen a strange bird in the forest. This bird was covered with wampum beads. Immediately, a hunting party was organized, and the hunters set out to try and capture this wonderful bird. The bird was as the hunter had described it—covered with white and purple feathers. All of the hunters tried to hit the bird with their arrows. Occasionally, the bird was hit by an arrow, and off would fly a shower of wampum. New wampum appeared on the bird to take the place of the fallen wampum. Finally, after trying to hit the bird for some time, the best hunters began to get discouraged, and one by one, they gave up trying to get the bird.

The young Wampanoag captive, from the unfriendly nation, asked the chief if he could try his luck. The Mohawk warriors did not want this to happen, and even threatened the boy's life. The chief interferred [*sic*], and told the boy that he could try. "If warriors have tried and failed, surely a mere boy cannot bring down the bird," said the chief.

The warriors finally agreed, and the boy lifted his bow and fitted an arrow. The swift arrow pierced the heart of the bird, and it fell to the earth. Its wampum plumage enriched the people. The boy married the chief's daughter, and with the marriage came peace between the two nations. The boy said, "Wampum shall bring and bind peace and it shall take the place of blood."

The Mohawk believed in a religion that saw life-forces in many forms, such as in animals, natural phenomena, and some special objects. These entities all had power, called *orenda* (o-REN-da). Any animal, object, or force that had orenda was capable of affecting humans. For this reason, people had to treat all entities with care and respect. Because spirit beings gave good things to people, the Mohawk believed that they were obliged to honor the spirit world.

Even though orenda ultimately came from the supernatural realm, people could make use of it to ensure their health and good fortune. Certain people had special abilities to use powers for the benefit of others. These people conducted rituals for individual and community well-being.

The fulfillment of one's dreams was also considered necessary to achieve and maintain health and success. According to the Mohawk's beliefs, dreams were expressions of a person's innermost thoughts and desires. The Mohawk thought that illness could be caused by thwarting the desires expressed in one's dreams. They believed, therefore, that in order to remain healthy or be cured from illness, all people needed to fulfill their dreams' wishes. The desires expressed in some dreams were obvious. For example, if a person dreamed of visiting someone or receiving a particular object, she or he satisfied the desire by making the visit or requesting the item seen in the dream. However, the messages in some

dreams were more difficult to interpret. In these cases, the dreamers consulted people who had special powers to interpret a dream's hidden or symbolic meanings. All community members were obliged to help a dreamer fulfill her or his wish. This practice emphasized the interdependence and mutual aid binding people together.

Some illnesses, though, were not related to one's dreams but rather to actions of witches. Witches were believed to be jealous or angry men and women who inflicted harm on others. They had several methods of causing sickness or death. They might secretly put dangerous concoctions into a victim's food or drink. Or they might use rituals and prayers to carry out their intentions. The Mohawk also believed that witches had the power to transform themselves into animals so that they could wander near their victims without arousing suspicion.

The Mohawk celebrated many kinds of rituals, including seasonal ceremonies concerned with foods and crops, curing ceremonies, and death rites. Seasonal ceremonies occurred in a specific sequence, following a yearly cycle or calendar. The timing and planning of calendrics was organized by Keepers of the Faith, a group of men and women who were among the most respected people in the community.

Each calendric ceremony was composed of several separate rites. The first rite in all ceremonials was a thanksgiving speech offered to supernatural and natural beings and forces. These entities were mentioned and thanked in a special order. Things closest to the earth, such as plants and animals, were noted first. Celestial entities, such as the wind, the sun, and the stars, were mentioned next. The list ended with supernatural beings and the Creator.

After the recitation of thanksgiving, tobacco was sprinkled on a fire as an invocation to spirits. The Mohawk believed that smoke from burning tobacco carried messages to the supernatural realm. Next, a group of rituals associated with each specific ceremonial was performed. At the end of the ceremonial, thanksgivings again were offered to supernatural and natural beings and followed by a communal feast, which often focused on the particular food associated with the occasion.

The first ceremonial of the year was Midwinter, which marked both the end of one year and the beginning of the next. Midwinter was the longest and most complex Mohawk ceremonial. It incorporated elements of thanksgiving, renewal, rejoicing, and preparation for the cycle of natural occurrences and human activities.

Midwinter lasted for nine days, each of which was devoted to performing certain rites. In the initial rite, a pure white dog was ritually strangled and burned. Like tobacco smoke, smoke from the burning dog carcass was thought to carry people's messages to spirits. Because dogs are loyal to their human owners, the animals symbolized the Mohawk's own loyalty to supernatural beings. After the "white dog

sacrifice," messengers called Our Uncles went through each house in the village to announce the start of Midwinter. While inside, a messenger took a large wooden paddle and stirred the ashes in every hearth. This rite represented the renewal of the community and the awakening of life-forces for the coming year.

After this beginning, several days were devoted to interpreting and fulfilling individual dreams. People went from house to house asking others to guess their dreams by interpreting hints or riddles provided by the dreamer. Each guesser offered an item that she or he believed was seen in the dream. When someone presented the correct object, the dreamer kept the item and returned all others to their original owners. The Mohawk's dream-guessing rituals were lively and entertaining. They released the tension and boredom that often set in during the long, cold winter.

The next section of Midwinter consisted of the Four Sacred Rituals. These included a Feather Dance, Thanksgiving Dance, Personal Chants, and a Bowl Game. To conclude Midwinter, the people performed dances for Our Life Supporters, offering thanks to the spirits of corn, beans, and squash, on whom the Mohawk depended for their survival.

Other calendric ceremonies also concentrated on events in the annual cycle. Their sequence was timed to changes in the natural environment or to people's economic activities. The Mohawk performed ceremonies dedicated to the sun and thunder, which provide warmth and rain to make plants grow. Other calendric rites were focused on the crops that the Mohawk produced. The rites were performed in the following order each year:

MAPLE: when sap begins to flow in maple trees;
SUN: when the sun's rays are warm in the spring;
THUNDER: when the spring thunder is heard, ushering in heavy rains that moisten the earth;
SEED PLANTING: when it is time to plant;
STRAWBERRY: when wild strawberries are ripe to eat;
BEAN: when the green beans are grown;
GREEN CORN: when the first corn is ripe;
HARVEST: when all the crops are harvested.

In addition to calendrics, the Mohawk performed curing rituals. Sick people frequently prescribed their own treatment based on their interpretations of their dreams. If they dreamed about a curing ceremony, they would request that the same rite be performed. Other types of curing rituals were conducted by members of "medicine societies." Each society had its own distinctive ceremonial cures. The choice of the society and the method of treatment were usually made by a specialist skilled in making diagnoses. This healer gave her or his opinion based on the patient's

symptoms, dreams, or hidden messages observed in bowls of water or tea. Healers looked into the liquids and tried to see movement or signs coming from supernatural forces. Then members of the medicine society performed their rituals in the patient's house. Some cures included massaging the patient with ashes from hearths. Like the stirring of ashes at the start of Midwinter, this act, too, functioned as a metaphor for renewal.

A 20th-century drawing of a Mohawk medicine woman.

A CURING RITUAL

Harmen van den Bogaert, a Dutch visitor to Mohawk territory, recorded the following account of a curing ritual he witnessed in 1635.

I saw a dozen men together who were going to drive off the devil. The floor of [the] house was thickly covered with the bark of trees for the hunters of the devil to walk upon. They were mostly old men, and they had their faces all painted with red paint—which they always do when they are going to do anything unusual. In the middle of the house they then put a man who was very sick. Close by sat an old woman with a turtle shell in her hands. In the turtle shell were a good many beads. She kept clinking all the while, and all of them sang to the measure; then they would proceed to catch the devil and trample him to death; they trampled the bark to atoms so that none of it remained whole; they beat at it in great amazement and then they blew that dust at one another; and after long stamping and running one of them went to the sick man and took away an otter that he had in his hands; and [one curer] sucked the sick man for awhile in his neck and on the back, and after that he spat in the otter's mouth and threw it down. Then they commenced to throw fire and eat fire, and kept scattering hot ashes and red-hot coal in such a way that I ran out of the house.

In other cures, healers donned masks representing supernatural beings whose restorative powers were applied to a patient. Masks had great spiritual meaning to the Mohawk. Some masks, called false faces, were made of wood and were associated with the spirits of the forest. Others, made of cornhusks, were linked to agricultural spirits. Masks were thought to be alive. They were carved into a living tree and extracted from the tree only when completed so that they retained the tree's life-forces. To keep their false faces alive, the Mohawk periodically "fed" the masks tobacco.

Another major group of ceremonies was associated with death. Funerals were held within a few days of a person's death and were marked by condolence speeches given by members of the moiety to which the deceased did not belong. Condolences expressed sadness and sympathy for the bereaved relatives. Societal balance and interdependence were symbolized by the obligations each moiety fulfilled in conducting funerals for the other group. The occasion of a person's death thus provided an opportunity for a communal expression of unity.

For 10 days after a death, food was set out for the deceased's ghost, which was believed to remain nearby. Then, to release the dead person's spirit, the Tenth-day Feast was held. During this rite, the personal possessions of the deceased were distributed among the guests. People believed that only after such a feast could a ghost begin its journey along the Milky Way to the afterworld.

In addition to marking individual deaths, the Mohawk conducted a ceremony once or twice a year to commemorate everyone who had died since the last such rite. Special songs and dances were performed to honor the dead and comfort the living.

Several themes were common to all Mohawk rituals. The theme of renewal of life and health is expressed in Midwinter, in seasonal calendrics, and in curing ceremonies. Thanksgivings to the natural and supernatural worlds, which are recited at the beginning and end of all ceremonies, demonstrate the importance of mutual respect and reciprocity among all creatures and forces of the universe. Finally, death rites recognize bonds between the living and the dead.

In daily life, the Mohawk lived according to ethics of hospitality, generosity, and consideration for others. These principles were shown in the people's eagerness to share with others whatever foods or goods they possessed. They gave aid and comfort to each other in times of crisis. And they believed that people should live harmoniously and respect all others' rights.

Unity was important in the political life of the Mohawk and their Iroquoian neighbors. Councils met periodically in each village and nation to discuss events of importance, plan communal activities, commemorate deaths of prominent people, and welcome visitors.

In the 14th or 15th century, the Mohawk formed the Iroquois Confederacy with the Oneida, the Onondaga, the Cayuga, and the Seneca. Also known as the Five Nations and the Iroquois League, the confederacy's main purpose was to preserve peace among members. It was a complex organization designed to respect each nation's rights but also to make them responsible for reciprocal aid in times of trouble. The confederacy was symbolized by a great longhouse stretching from east to west across Iroquois territory. In the Mohawk language, it was called *Ganonsyonni* (ga-non-SHON-ni), meaning "the extended house," or *Rotinonsyonni* (ro-di-non-SHON-ni), meaning "They are of the extended house." In this longhouse, the Mohawk were the Keepers of the Eastern Door, for theirs was the easternmost Iroquois nation.

Confederacy chiefs were men chosen by elder women, or matrons, of their clan. Chiefs and matrons attained

A meeting of the chiefs of the Iroquois Confederacy, depicted in a 1724 French engraving. The laws of the confederacy are recorded in the patterns of the wampum belt stretched before them.

their positions because of personal skills, intelligence, good judgment, and generosity. A chief was installed for life during a ceremony in which he was crowned with a headdress of deer antlers. If a chief's conduct in councils or even his behavior in the community was deemed inappropriate, he could be deposed by the matrons of his clan. These women first warned the man about his unsatisfactory behavior. Then, if their warnings went unheeded,

he was "dehorned"—impeached by removing his chiefly antler headdress.

According to Iroquois oral traditions, the confederacy was founded by two chiefs named Hiawatha (hi-ya-WA-ta) and Deganawida (de-ga-na-WEE-da). Hiawatha was originally from the Onondaga. Deganawida was born among the Huron Indians north of Lake Ontario. Both men, however, journeyed from their home to Mohawk territory and were later adopted by the

Mohawk. After Hiawatha and Deganawida met in a Mohawk village, they began to discuss the idea of a confederacy that would unite all five nations in a great peace. Deganawida then traveled to the other nations to submit the plan for their consent. The first evening, he stayed at the house of a Mohawk woman and told her of his purpose, which she approved. This episode in the story symbolized the necessity of gaining women's consent to actions taken by the league.

All of the Iroquois chiefs accepted the plan proposed by Deganawida and Hiawatha, except for a belligerent Onondaga leader named Thadodaho (ta-do-DA-ho). Thadodaho at last said that he would join after it was promised that he would be "first among equals." To show respect for Thadodaho and for Onondaga territory as the geographic center of Iroquois lands, league councils were always held in the principal Onondaga village. The Onondaga are therefore known as the "fire keepers." They had the honor of announcing council meetings.

Chiefs held confederacy meetings at least once a year, but they could meet whenever an important issue needed to be discussed. Councils were concerned with intertribal matters, trade negotiations with foreigners, and deliberations of war and peace.

There were originally 50 confederacy chiefs, each with a name or title that was passed on to another man of his clan after his death or demotion. However, two of the titles, those of the league's founders Deganawida (also known as the Peacemaker) and Hiawatha, were always left unfilled. Each nation had its own titles: The Onondaga had 14 titles, the Cayuga had 10, the Mohawk and the Oneida each had 9, and the Seneca had 8.

The Five Nations were divided into two moieties, paralleling the kinship division of clans. One moiety—the Elders—consisted of the Mohawk, the Onondaga, and the Seneca. The Oneida and the Cayuga constituted the other, or the Younger, moiety. Seating at council meetings was arranged by nation and moiety. The Mohawk and the Seneca sat on one side, the Oneida and the Cayuga sat on the other, and the Onondaga took the central position before the council fire.

All decisions of the confederacy had to be unanimous. In reaching a consensus, deliberations proceeded according to a fixed sequence of events. The topic of discussion was announced by the Onondaga, who then "gave" it to the Mohawk for their consideration. When they reached a decision, they passed the topic to the Seneca chiefs. After reaching their conclusions, the Seneca passed it back to the Mohawk, who announced their joint decision and relayed the topic "across the fire" to the other moiety. The Oneida and the Cayuga deliberated next, passing the matter between them. After the Oneida declared their decision to the Mohawk, a Mohawk chief announced the results to the Onondaga. If the Onondaga agreed, the decision was unanimous,

A portion of the second largest Iroquois wampum belt, named the To-ta-da-ho after one of the original chiefs of the confederacy. The series of white diamonds running down its center symbolizes the binding together of the Iroquois nations.

and the matter was settled with a final ceremonial declaration by Thadodaho. At the conclusion of a session, the actions of the council were "read into" the belts of wampum that record significant events. Woven patterns or images in the belts were mnemonic devices that helped people recall important agreements or historical episodes.

If a consensus was not achieved at a council meeting, the problem could be given back to the Mohawk for further deliberation, starting the process of negotiation once more. If unanimity was impossible to reach, the matter was set aside, and the council fire was covered up with ashes. This ritual act marked the inability of the league chiefs to "roll their words into one bundle." It was so important that all be of One Heart, One Mind, One Law that the league could take no action without unanimous agreement.

In addition to civil or peace chiefs, war chiefs from each nation had responsibility for discussing and planning military expeditions. These men could have their opinions heard through selected speakers at confederacy meetings, but they did not participate in decision making. Clan matrons or other prominent women could similarly appoint speakers to voice their opinions to the league chiefs.

This complex political structure achieved remarkable results over the course of several centuries. By the beginning of the 17th century, the Mohawk and the other Iroquois nations wielded considerable power in the Northeast, extending their influence far beyond their own territory. Skillful Iroquois diplomats negotiated agreements with other nations, backed up by the success of their warriors. And the league itself rested on a secure cultural foundation, sustained by the social and economic contributions of Iroquois women and men. ▲

A fanciful drawing by a 17th-century French artist of a tattooed Mohawk man. The turtle on his thigh probably represents the Indian's clan.

KEEPERS
OF THE
EASTERN DOOR

The beginning of the 18th century was a pivotal period for American Indians. Only a few Europeans had landed on the shores of North America. They came as traders, explorers, missionaries, and settlers. At first, Indians welcomed these newcomers—mostly because they wanted European trade goods. However, early immigrants from Europe were to bring much more to the Indians. In time, their arrival would prove to be the start of an overwhelming tide of change.

The Mohawk had had news of Europeans long before they met white men face-to-face. From other Indians they heard about new types of tools, utensils, clothing, and weapons that the Europeans offered in exchange for beaver furs. Europeans desired these furs in almost endless numbers because beaver hats and collars were the rage of fashion in 17th-century Holland, France, and Great Britain.

Involvement in this trade had both positive and negative effects on Indian cultures. On the positive side, it allowed the Indians to improve their living conditions in several ways. For the first time, they obtained goods made of metal, such as iron kettles, knives, scissors, nails, axes, and sword blades. They also used iron hinges to fasten shelves in their longhouses. Metal objects were more durable than the earthen pottery and stone or bone implements that native people had previously made and used. Woolen cloth from European factories was also greatly desired by Indians. The Mohawk especially liked the heavy duffel cloth sold at Dutch trading posts because it gave better protection against the frequent rains than did the beaver skins that people had traditionally worn. Although duffel cloth came in several colors, the Mohawk preferred subdued shades of blue or gray because

An iron axhead that was traded to the Mohawk by the French. The Indians prized European metal goods, which were much more durable than the stone tools they traditionally made.

these did not startle and frighten away animals in the forest.

The Mohawk so favored the tools and utensils brought by Europeans that they soon stopped learning traditional skills such as pottery making and tool-making. The goods that at first had been considered novelties and luxuries rapidly became necessities of life. The Mohawk's growing dependence on European goods forced them to alter their economy. In order to obtain trade items, men had to trap beaver in increasing numbers. Before European contact, the Mohawk had been careful to hunt only as many animals as they needed for food and clothing. Enough animals therefore survived and reproduced to ensure an adequate supply the next year. With growing desires for trade goods, however, people abandoned their efforts to conserve the animal population and instead began to trap many more animals than they had in the past.

In a very short time, all the beaver in the lands controlled by the Mohawk were gone. The situation was desperate; without beaver pelts people could not obtain the goods they now needed to perform their daily activities. Louis de Lahontan, a French traveler of the time, commented on the Mohawk's plight in his journal. He concluded that without beaver skins they "would be starved to death, or at least obliged to leave their country."

The Mohawk had two alternatives. One was to withdraw from trade. Such a choice was obviously unacceptable because it would have meant giving up those items that had improved their life. The second alternative was to try to obtain pelts from those Indian groups that still had an abundance of beaver in their territory. Since these peoples also

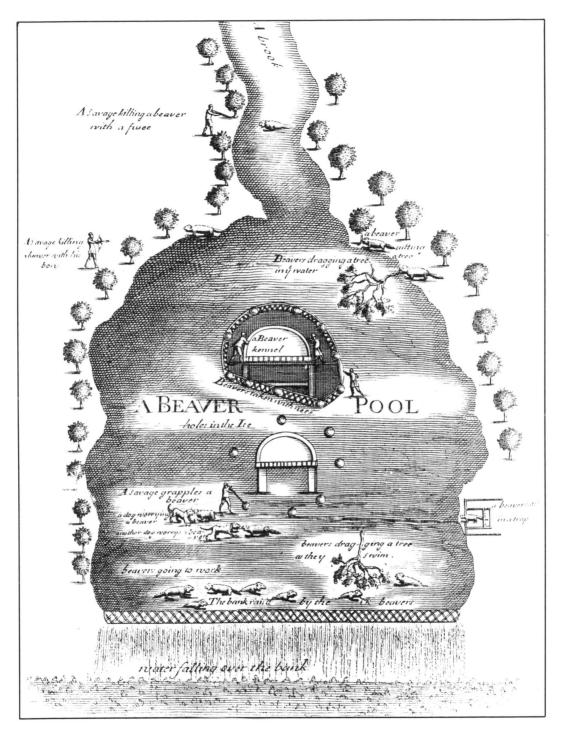

Within the engraving, the following labels appear:

a brook

A Savage killing a beaver with a fusee

A Savage killing a beaver with his bow

Beavers dragging a tree in ye water

a beaver cutting a tree

a Beaver kennel

A BEAVER POOL

holes in the Ice

Beavers taken with nets

A Savage grapples a beaver

a dog worrying a beaver

another dog worry: a beaver

beavers going to work

beavers dragging a tree as they swim

a beaver in a trap

The bank raised by the beavers

water falling over the bank

An 18th-century English engraving of Iroquois men hunting beavers. Among the hunting tools they used were guns, bows and arrows, trained dogs, traps, and nets.

wanted to trade animal skins to Europeans, the Mohawk were compelled to obtain the skins by force. And so began decades of intense intertribal warfare.

One of the first major conflicts occurred in the summer of 1609, when a group of Mohawk warriors were attacked by a contingent of Huron Indians, Algonkian Indians, and French soldiers led by French explorer Samuel de Champlain. The Huron and the Algonkians were already enemies of the Mohawk. The two groups had previously entered into alliances with France and sought French aid in a campaign against the Mohawk.

The Indian and French allies set out against a Mohawk force that was rumored to be near a large lake, later to be known as Lake Champlain. The two groups of warriors met on July 29, 1609. Champlain's force, made up of approximately 60 men, was largely outnumbered by the 200 Mohawk fighters led by 3 chiefs. According to Indian custom, the enemies approached each other and began shooting their arrows. Champlain and his men, however, surprised the Mohawk with something they had never seen before—muskets. Champlain opened fire on the Mohawk chiefs, killing two of them immediately. The third chief was wounded and died soon afterward.

The Mohawk were terrified by the sound of guns and by the instantaneous deaths that they caused. As Champlain's men continued to shoot, the Indians fled for their life. Champlain was

satisfied with the success of this battle because he mistakenly believed that it proved French superiority and confirmed that his force's victory over the Mohawk was inevitable.

In the following year, Mohawk warriors fought against another group of Algonkians and French troops at a place

An engraving of French explorer Samuel de Champlain's attack on the Mohawk in 1609. The illustration is often attributed to Champlain.

near the Richelieu River in present-day Quebec. Again French soldiers used muskets, killing as many as 100 Mohawk men. And again the Indians fled in fear of the guns' deadly effect. Although the Mohawk were alarmed at the outcome of these battles, they were not to be easily dislodged from their lands or dissuaded from trying to tighten their control over trade.

At this time, more and more French were gathering along the St. Lawrence River in the north. Meanwhile, Dutch traders were establishing posts near the Hudson River in present-day New York State. The principal Dutch post, opened in 1615, was called Fort Orange. (The fort would be renamed Albany by the British in 1664.) It was located near the territories of both the Mohawk and the Mahican Indians. War broke out almost immediately between these two Indian peoples for control over access to the fort. Both groups wanted to stop other Indians from trading directly with Dutch merchants. They each hoped to increase their own power by forcing others to trade through them as go-betweens. After the wars ended in 1619 with Mohawk victories, the Mohawk replaced the Mahican as the main suppliers of beaver pelts to Dutch dealers. Meanwhile, the Iroquois Confederacy had signed a commercial treaty with the Dutch in 1618. Although the agreement concerned all five Iroquois Nations, the Mohawk figured particularly prominently in dealings with Dutch traders because their territory was closest to Fort Orange.

Dutch suppliers introduced the Mohawk to a wide range of foreign products. Metalware, such as brass kettles and iron hunting tools, was especially desired. In addition, the Mohawk obtained duffel cloth, biscuits, and flour. They also traded with the Dutch for wampum, which was of great ceremo-nial value to the Iroquois. Wampum was produced by the Montauk, Shinnecock, and other Indian peoples living on what is now Long Island, New York, then a territory colonized by Dutch merchants and settlers. The Dutch contracted with Long Island Indians to increase their production of wampum because it was in such high demand by the Iroquois.

Warfare between the Mohawk and the Mahican erupted again in the mid-1620s, ending in 1628 with another Mohawk victory. During this period, tensions in the area had increased due to encroachments of Dutch settlers on Indian lands around Fort Orange. As colonists arrived in greater numbers, Indians and Europeans began to compete more than ever for farmland and hunting areas. At the same time, the beaver population in eastern and central New York continued to decline because of heavy hunting, which in turn increased intertribal competition.

A Mohawk leader expressed his nation's dilemma in a conversation with Dutch officials in 1659:

> The Dutch say we are brothers, and joined together with chains, but that lasts only as long as we have beavers; after that no attention is paid to us.

The "attention" that the Mohawk wanted was access to European products, and they were prepared to secure trade by engaging in warfare against their neighbors. Intense conflicts raged in the region from the 1630s through the 1650s. Mohawk raids during this period included attacks against the Pequot and the Narragansett in New England, the Huron in southern Ontario, the Montagnais near Tadoussac in northeastern Quebec, the Abenaki and Maliseet in the Maritime Provinces, the Ottawa and Algonquins in the Ottawa River valley, and the Neutral and Erie in the Great Lakes regions. In all these areas, the Mohawk and their Iroquois allies were victorious. They compelled other native peoples to supply them with furs and to deal with European traders through them. One tactic the Mohawk used was to set up ambushes along the Hudson and St. Lawrence rivers, attacking travelers who carried animal skins en route to the trading posts at Fort Orange, Montreal, or Quebec. The Mohawk were so successful that they were able to take as much as one-quarter of the furs transported by other people along the rivers. As a result, some groups, such as the Huron, Neutral, and Erie, were forced to flee from their ancestral lands, most of them eventually relocating farther to the west. Mohawk prowess was enhanced when Dutch traders began selling guns to them in the 1640s, giving the Mohawk an advantage unavailable to other Indians at that time.

In addition to the turmoil created by armed conflict, the mid-17th century witnessed incalculable Indian deaths from the ravages of European diseases. When Europeans arrived in North America, they unwittingly brought with them germs that caused epidemics of deadly diseases such as smallpox and measles. Because these viruses were not native to North America, Indian populations had never developed immunities to them. Therefore, when the germs were introduced to the Indians through contact with Europeans, the organisms' deadly force was impossible to withstand. Within a few decades, thousands of Indians in the Northeast had died. Families and sometimes entire villages were destroyed in a single epidemic.

During this time, the Mohawk had increased their involvement with Europeans. Commercial dealings with Dutch traders were expanded after the Mohawk's victories over other Indian groups. Second, the Mohawk also traded with British merchants, who were enlarging their sphere of influence and attempting to wrest control over commerce from the Dutch. In addition, the tribe periodically established contacts with French merchants in Montreal and Quebec.

By 1640, only about 1,000 Dutch people had settled in all of the colony of New Netherland and perhaps 100 in the vicinity of Fort Orange. But within a few years, settlement increased rapidly. Because the soil in Mohawk territory was rich and productive, it was desired by Dutch farmers for crops and orchards. The Dutch government then adopted an official policy of purchasing land fairly from the Indians. They were vitally interested in establishing and maintaining good trade relations with Indian groups and did not want to an-

A 1630 map of the Dutch colony of New Netherland.

ger them by allowing unscrupulous land dealings. But despite official intentions, Dutch settlers tried to occupy Indian land without legally purchasing it. In the 1650s, the Dutch set up local courts for administering their colonies and heard many complaints brought by Mohawk people against illegal expansion of Dutch farms into their territory.

British settlers also made inroads into eastern and central New York from their areas of colonization in New England. In 1664, the British took control of lands claimed by the Dutch as well, owing to British victories in conflicts with Holland fought both in North America and in Europe. In the same year, Mohawk and Seneca representatives concluded a commercial agreement with British merchants, pledging to shift their allegiance to the English.

However, new hostilities were soon created by the movement of British settlers into Mohawk territory. Great Britain at first allowed settlers to negotiate land deals with the Indians without official supervision. The settlers did not always deal fairly with the natives, and the resulting tensions increased as more English immigrants arrived. In some cases, Mohawk individuals sought British aid by turning their land over to the jurisdiction of the Crown. The British government then assumed legal responsibility for safeguarding Mohawk land rights. But this maneuver did not solve the problem, because local officials sometimes disobeyed policies set down in London.

In the early 1690s, colonial governors tried to encourage more settlement by granting lands within Mohawk territory to English citizens. Then, in 1696, the British appointed a commissioner to record colonial land transactions, including those between Indians and settlers. The following year, two Mohawks brought a serious complaint to the commissioner, declaring that they had been tricked into signing a deed granting an Englishman control over some of their land. The fraudulent deed covered an enormous area, extending for 50 miles on both sides of the Mohawk River west of Albany. According to the Indians' testimony, Godfrey Dellius, a minister living in their community, had advised them that they should appoint him as their guardian to protect their land. The two Mohawks stated that they then signed a document that they thought was the agreement of guardianship but turned out to be a deed of sale. The Indians' claim was recognized as just, and the land deal was annulled.

Perhaps because of the huge amount of land involved, injustice in this incident was brought to light. But most likely many other fraudulent deals went undetected and unredressed. Thousands of acres of Mohawk land were undoubtedly stolen by similar means. Colonial administrators often helped in this process. Many members of local assemblies were themselves wealthy landowners. They were in a position to establish policies and make decisions from which they could benefit financially at the expense of Indian peoples.

Despite these serious problems, the Mohawk remained loyal to their British allies. They continued to trade with the British and aid them in battles against the enemies of England, most notably France. But even though the Mohawk were the enemies of the French in military matters, the Indians wanted to establish commercial relations with them. In 1653, representatives of the two groups signed a treaty guaranteeing the peaceful flow of valuables. Still, the Mohawk preferred trading with the British because British goods were of superior quality to those of the French and could be obtained at a lower cost. In fact, one of the Mohawk's motives in signing treaties with the French was to put pressure on British merchants to keep their prices low. The Mohawk reasoned that if the two European groups had to compete with each other for Indian trade, neither one could exert monopoly control. By negotiating agreements with both powers, the Mohawk demonstrated their skill at developing strategies by which they would prosper economically.

The arrival of French missionaries also increased contact between the Mohawk and the French traders. In the early 1600s, missionaries from France began to contact Indians in the Northeast. Jesuit priests first took up missionary work in 1610, visiting Algonkian and Huron allies of the French. The Mohawk did not encounter missionaries until 1642. In that year, a Catholic priest named Isaac Jogues made a journey to their territory in hopes of establishing a mission there but the trip was not successful. When Jogues departed from the region, he carelessly left behind a black box, which he had probably used as a storage container.

During the next four years, waves of disease struck the Mohawk communities Jogues had visited. Crops had also failed. Because the Mohawk believed that disease could be caused by witchcraft, they attributed their illnesses to the black box. In the words of another French priest, Father Gabriel Lalemant, the Mohawk came to the following conclusion:

> Sickness having fallen upon their bodies after [Jogues's] departure, and worms having perhaps damaged their corn, these poor blind creatures have believed that the Father had left them the Demon among them, and that all our discourses aimed only to exterminate them.

Although Jogues did not knowingly cause harm to the Mohawk, he may actually have been a carrier of the deadly smallpox virus that spread rapidly among their villagers. Believing the priest was responsible for the disasters that struck them, the Mohawk executed Jogues when he returned to their village in 1646. Members of the Wolf and Turtle clans opposed the execution, but it was carried out by Bear clan leaders nonetheless. And although Jogues's death caused renewed friction between the Mohawk and French, Father Lalemant observed:

> It is true that, speaking humanly, these Barbarians have apparent reasons for reproaching us—inasmuch as the scourges which humble the proud precede us or accompany us wherever we go.

Despite setbacks, Jesuit missionaries returned to Mohawk territory in 1656 and 1657. At that time, the Mohawk actively encouraged these visits. In fact, when priests proposed journeys to the Iroquois Nations, both the Mohawk and Onondaga suggested that they build the first French mission among the Iroquois in their territory. These nations recognized that friendship with the Jesuits would be well regarded by French officials and could strengthen commercial agreements. At an official meeting between the Iroquois and the missionaries in Quebec, the Onondaga claimed that the priests should come to them because they had

A 19th-century engraving of a French Jesuit missionary preaching to the Iroquois. In the 1650s, the Mohawk encouraged the Jesuits to establish missions in their territories because they hoped the presence of these priests would solidify their trading relationship with the French.

been the first to start negotiations about the missions. When it was the Mohawk's turn to speak, they invoked the symbolic metaphor of the confederacy as a longhouse and of the Mohawk as Keepers of the Eastern Door. A Mohawk orator, quoted by Father Joseph LeMerciér, declared:

> Ought not one to enter a house by the door, and not by the chimney or roof of the cabin, unless he be a thief, and wish to take the inmates by surprise? We, the Five Iroquois Nations, compose but one cabin; we maintain but one fire; and we have, from time immemorial, dwelt under the same roof. Well, then, will you not enter the cabin by the door? It is with us Anniehronnons [Mohawk], that you should begin; whereas you, by beginning with the Onnontaehronnon [Onondaga], try to enter by the roof and through the chimney.

Despite the eloquence of this argument, the Jesuits established missions among the Onondaga. But later, in 1656, they traveled to Mohawk territory.

On the whole, missionary efforts to convert Mohawks met with very limited success. Only a few natives listened seriously to the priests' sermons. The Mohawk's motives in welcoming the priests had been more economic than religious. They had wanted to establish themselves as intermediaries in French commerce and hoped to compel members of the other four Iroquois Nations to trade through them. Intertribal competition therefore occasionally spread within the Iroquois Confederacy as well as between the Iroquois and other Indian groups.

Nevertheless, missionaries offered advice to French officials about how best to maintain Mohawk friendship. Even though the Mohawk lacked enthusiasm for religious conversion, the priests' statements about the Indians and their culture were favorable while peace lasted. Father Simon Le Moyne, who visited Mohawk villages in 1656 and 1657, commented:

> No hospitals are needed among them, because there are neither mendicants nor paupers as long as there are any rich people among them. Their kindness, humanity, and courtesy not only make them liberal with what they have, but cause them to possess hardly anything except in common. A whole village must be without corn before any individual can be obliged to endure privation.

When the fragile peace turned to war, as often happened, the Jesuits' remarks also turned bitter. They counseled the government to step up attacks against the Mohawk. They advised that if the Mohawk could be defeated, the other four Iroquois nations would abandon war and agree to treaties with France. The Mohawk, however, remained unbeaten, and the Jesuits were compelled to write with respect, if not approval, of Mohawk military skills. In 1660, Fa-

A French map drawn by a Jesuit in the 1650s showing the territory of the five Iroquois nations.

ther Lalemant offered the following review:

> The Agnieronnons [Mohawk] have had to fight with all their neighbors—with the Abnaquois [Abenaki], who are eastward of them; on the south with the Andastogehronnons [Andastes], a people inhabiting the shores of Virginia; with the Hurons on the west; and with all the Algonkian nations scattered throughout the north. But what is more astonishing is that they actually hold dominion over 500 leagues around, although their numbers are small; for the Agnieronnons do not exceed 500 men able to bear arms, who occupy three or four villages.

During a period of intensifying warfare in the 1660s, French forces organized a strike against Mohawk villages. An army of 1,200 French troops and 600 Indian allies under the leadership of Marquis Prouville de Tracy entered Mohawk territory. Advance word arrived in time to warn villagers, who fled to the forests for safety. French soldiers then burned the empty houses and surrounding cornfields.

A further complication in relations between the Mohawk and Europeans was set in motion in 1667 when Jesuits persuaded several Mohawk converts to leave their ancestral lands and resettle in missions near Montreal. The priests argued that because the converts were distrusted by their relatives and neighbors, they might become targets of retaliation as warfare intensified. The missionaries further claimed that Christian Mohawk would be safe only near French forts. After listening to these arguments, a group of Catholic Mohawk established a new village on the south side of the St. Lawrence River at La Prairie. Attracting Mohawk and Oneida Indians, the settlement's population grew throughout the 1670s. In 1676, it was moved upriver to Sault St. Louis (present-day Lachine Rapids) because the soil at La Prairie was too damp for growing corn. The village was renamed Kahnawake (gah-na-WA-ge), meaning "at the rapids." The appellation had symbolic significance for these people because it had previously been the name of a Mohawk village in what is now New York State.

The Mohawk remaining in New York were alarmed by the departure of the Christians for several reasons. First, it was a sign of a deep rift in Mohawk unity. Because the Mohawk valued the principle of One Heart, One Mind, One Law, such a split was especially disturbing. Second, many Mohawk worried that the French would exercise political as well as religious influence over the converts. They feared that the French would persuade the Christian Indians to fight against their kin. This worry was well founded. Kahnawake Mohawk initially pledged neutrality in Iroquois-French conflicts, but they were often drawn into battles on the side of France. They also traveled as ambassadors to the Mohawk in New York, where they tried, without success, to convince their kin to stop fighting the French and instead take up arms against British forces.

During this period, another mission for Mohawk Indians was established by an order of French Sulpician priests. In 1676, they founded the village of Kanesatake (ga-ne-sa-DA-ge) on the island of Montreal. The settlement was soon relocated to land a short distance west of Montreal along the Ottawa River, where it has remained since. The new site was favored by French authorities because it gave them a friendly post on the Ottawa River leading to the Great Lakes. Converts at Kanesatake were from various Iroquoian and Algonkian groups, but the majority were Mohawk. They, too, sometimes fought against their former neighbors.

At both Kahnawake and Kanesatake, people attempted to continue with their traditional way of life as much as possible. They succeeded in maintaining their native economies and clan systems. However, they abandoned several customs that were criticized by Jesuit teachings. Jesuits stressed the importance of marital bonds and therefore condemned the Mohawk custom of allowing couples to divorce easily. They also opposed the Indians' tendency to indulge their children. Instead, they preached that children must be obedient and should be punished if they misbehaved. Finally, the priests tried to eradicate Mohawk beliefs about the importance of interpreting and fulfilling one's dreams. To Jesuit thinking, these practices were signs of devil worship. Over the next few decades, converts were influenced by the missionaries' teachings and gradually adopted European values. These changes, of course, made converts appear strange to the Mohawk remaining in New York and gave further evidence of French treachery.

Meanwhile, despite the alliance between the Mohawk and the British, conflicts increased as the number of En-

glish settlers grew and as their appetite for land seemed to become insatiable. In the early years of contact, Indians had far outnumbered the newcomers. But in a relatively short time, the balance shifted because of the extraordinarily high rate of Indian deaths from disease and the huge number of immigrants from Europe. When the English first arrived in North America, they needed the help of Indians for their survival. But as early as 1684, less than 80 years after the first English settlement was established in North America, an Iroquois chief made the fol-

The Mohawk village of Kahnawake in 1722.

lowing remark to Colonel Thomas Dongan, a British official in Albany:

> You are a mighty sachem [leader] and
> we but a small people. When the
> English first came to New York,
> Virginia and Maryland, they were but
> a small people and we a large nation,
> and we finding they were good
> people gave them land and dealt
> civilly by them; Now that you are
> grown numerous and we decreased,
> you must protect us from the French.

Even though the Mohawk remained allied to the British, they distrusted British motives and feared that their lands would be taken by colonists. The Indians also were uneasy about the lack of full British support in campaigns against French forces. Needing to protect their own safety, the Mohawk negotiated several peace treaties with the French. Although these treaties were soon dissolved by actions on both sides, British officials were threatened by any sign of Mohawk friendship with France. At a meeting in 1691 between the Mohawk and Colonel Henry Sloughter, governor of New York, the Englishman reproached the Indians with "You must keep the Enemy in perpetual alarm." To this, a Mohawk leader responded, "Why don't you say, '*We* will keep the Enemy in perpetual alarm.' "

In the same year, the Mohawk were given proof of the validity of their complaints. A force of British and Iroquois warriors attacked French forts in Montreal in August 1691. But because the British had not sent enough troops to counteract French forces, the campaign was unsuccessful, and the Mohawk lost a large number of men.

At a meeting held in 1692 with Governor Richard Ingoldsby, who replaced Sloughter after the colonel's death, the Mohawk repeated their misgivings about British intentions. Their speeches told of their predicament:

> We are all subjects of one great King
> and Queen, we have one head, one
> heart, one interest, and are all
> engaged in the same war. We are
> resolved to carry on the war, though
> we know we only are in danger of
> being losers. Pray do you prosecute
> the war with the same resolution.
> You are strong and have many
> people. You have a great king who is
> able to hold out long. We are but a
> small people, declining daily, by the
> men we lose in this war, we do our
> utmost to destroy the enemy; but
> how strange does it seem to us! How
> unaccountable! that while our great
> king is so inveterate against the
> French, and you so earnest with us to
> carry on the war, that powder is now
> sold dearer to us than ever? We are
> poor, and not able to buy while we
> neglect hunting; and we cannot hunt
> and carry on the war at the same
> time. You desire us to keep the
> Enemy in perpetual alarm; Is it not to
> secure your own frontiers? Why then
> not one word of your people that are
> to join us? How comes it that none of
> our Brethren fastened in the same

chain with us, offer their helping hand in this general war? Pray make plain to us this mystery? How can they and we be subjects of the same great king, and not be engaged in the same war?

The same year, 600 French troops under Count Louis de Frontenac attacked several Mohawk villages. One of Frontenac's motives was to show the Mohawk that they could not depend on the British for protection. He was correct. French soldiers were able to destroy 3 villages and capture 300 prisoners, including 100 warriors and 200 noncombatant men, women, and children.

By the end of the 17th century, turmoil in the Northeast continued unabated. The Mohawk and their Iroquois allies renewed attacks against several Indian peoples. They ranged as far west as Lake Superior in raids against the Huron, Neutral, and Petun, who had relocated there. They made expeditions to the south as well, reaching to Virginia and the Carolinas.

The turn of the 18th century also witnessed increasing expansion of British colonies, which encroached ever more on Mohawk territory. The situation of Indian peoples grew steadily more difficult. Skilled strategists among the Mohawk attempted to work out some alignment of forces so that they could remain independent of both the British and French. Although they were successful for a time, stability for the Mohawk was to be short-lived. ▲

The great Mohawk chief and orator Joseph Brant tried to persuade the Iroquois Confederacy to side with the British during the American Revolution.

4

DEEPENING CRISES

At the beginning of the 18th century, the Mohawk retained their dominance over Indian groups in the Northeast. Many of their enemies had been defeated, forced to abandon their territories and resettle farther west. Others remained in the east but pledged not to take up arms against the Iroquois. Some were compelled to pay symbolic tribute in wampum to the Mohawk who represented the victorious confederacy. The league itself remained strong. The Iroquois were well respected by European powers as much for their skillful diplomacy as for their military success. In 1720, Pierre Charlevoix, a French Recollet priest, observed:

> As the Iroquois were situated between us [French] and the English, they soon found that both would be under the necessity of keeping well with them; and indeed it has been the chief care of both colonies, to gain

them over to their own party, or, at least, to persuade them to stand neutral: and as they were persuaded that if either of these nations should entirely get the ascendant over the other, they must soon be subjected themselves; they have found the secret of balancing their success; and if we reflect that their whole force united has never exceeded five or six thousand combatants, and that it is a great while since they have diminished more than one half, we must needs allow, they must have used infinite abilities and address.

But the previous 100 years had taken a heavy toll on the Mohawk Nation. Many Mohawk had been killed, both from deadly European diseases and from the scourge of warfare that continued without respite. The land of the People of the Place of Flint was diminished in size as the Dutch and British colonies expanded. Because of these difficult conditions, many Mohawk Indians left their traditional lands, migrating northward to the protected missions at Kahnawake and Kanesatake near Montreal.

In the second year of the 18th century, the Iroquois Confederacy signed a peace treaty with French representatives in Quebec. However, like all the others before it, the treaty was soon torn apart. Hostilities in Europe led to war in North America. In 1702, Queen Anne's War erupted between Great Britain and France. As in past conflicts, this war engulfed the Indians, who were pressured into aiding their respective allies. During the war, which lasted until 1713, the Iroquois fought on the side of the English. France had the help of several Algonkian peoples. The majority of the Mohawk were loyal to the British, but French leaders in Quebec persuaded the Catholic Mohawk at Kahnawake and Kanesatake to aid their cause. Deep divisions within the Mohawk Nation grew when relatives and former neighbors fought on different sides.

As Queen Anne's War continued, the British government wanted to strengthen its alliance with the Iroquois. In an attempt to win favor, Protestant missionaries from England began working in Indian communities in the early 18th century. The British saw that the Catholic Mohawk had shifted their allegiance from Great Britain to France, so they hoped that good relations between the British ministers and the Mohawk communities would increase the Indians' support for Britain. Several missions were established, but none attracted any strong interest from the Mohawk in that period.

In another attempt to encourage goodwill, the British sponsored a trip to England in 1710 by the so-called Four Indian Kings. Three of these "kings" were prominent Mohawk leaders, including a chief known as Hendrick, who became an important ally in later British wars. The kings were entertained in London, where they met with British officials and had an audience with Queen Anne. At the meeting, Indian leaders asked the queen for protection from French attacks. She responded by ordering the construction of a new fort and chapel, called Fort Hunter, along the Mohawk River.

Although Fort Hunter provided security against French raids, it did nothing to stop encroachment on Mohawk land by British colonists. In fact, the presence of Fort Hunter encouraged settlement by Europeans because, living near the fort, they felt protected. In the previous century, the westernmost colonial communities had been located near Schenectady, but by 1720, larger numbers of settlers had moved farther west. During the next decade, many German immigrants also invaded the Mohawk and Hudson River valleys. This new wave of immigration encroached on native communities. The city of Albany itself laid fraudulent claim to nearby Mohawk territory. Fearing that all their land would be occupied by settlers, the Mohawk in 1733 turned

Sa Ga Yeath Qua Pieth Tow, also known as Brant, was one of four Mohawk leaders invited to travel to London and meet with Queen Anne of England in 1710. This portrait by John Verelst was painted during the Mohawk's trip.

over a large tract of land—including 1,200 acres of meadow and 2,000 acres of forest—to the English king, George III. The agreement between the Mohawk and the king stipulated that neither could sell or transfer any of the land without the consent of the other.

The title page of a report of treaty negotiations between colonial officials and the leaders of the six Iroquois nations. The report was printed by Benjamin Franklin in 1746.

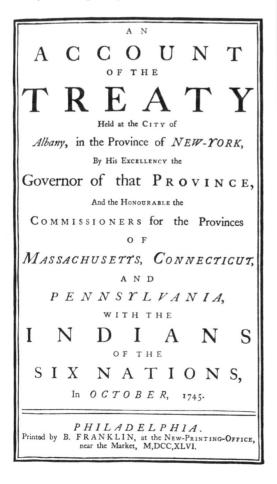

A N

ACCOUNT

OF THE

TREATY

Held at the CITY of

Albany, in the Province of *NEW-YORK*,

By His EXCELLENCY the

Governor of that PROVINCE,

And the HONOURABLE the

COMMISSIONERS for the Provinces

OF

MASSACHUSETTS, *CONNECTICUT*,

AND

PENNSYLVANIA,

WITH THE

INDIANS

OF THE

SIX NATIONS,

In *OCTOBER*, 1745.

PHILADELPHIA.

Printed by B. FRANKLIN, at the NEW-PRINTING-OFFICE, near the Market, M,DCC,XLVI.

The Mohawk hoped that their lands were finally safe from settlers' advances. However, the British government was either unable or unwilling to protect natives from illegal sales. Throughout the 1730s and 1740s, the Mohawk brought numerous complaints to local officials, asserting that colonists were moving into their territory. After a careful review of deeds, a British surveyor general, Cadwallader Colden, found that many of the documents transferred ownership of larger tracts of land than the Mohawk sellers had intended. Because the Indians were unfamiliar with European methods of measuring land and could not read the deeds, they were easily cheated out of hundreds and even thousands of acres. Colden recommended that Mohawk lands be properly measured and surveyed with Indians present in order to protect their rights.

During this period, the confederacy was enlarged by the addition of a sixth nation, the Tuscarora. The Tuscarora were Iroquoian peoples, closely related linguistically and culturally to the five original league members. At the time of European contact, they lived in present-day Virginia. Later, when English settlements there expanded into Indian territories, the Tuscarora sought refuge in the north. They asked for protection from the powerful Iroquois and were admitted to the confederacy in 1722.

In the following decades, British missionaries renewed attempts to con-

continued on page 65

YESTERDAY'S TRADITIONS TODAY

Like many other Indian tribes, the Mohawk take great pride in their craftspeople. By creating beautiful objects using the same techniques and materials as their ancestors, these master artisans provide a vital link to the past.

Beadwork is one of the Mohawk's most valued craft traditions. Long ago, tribespeople strung purple and white shell beads and wove the strings together to form valuable wampum belts. After the Mohawk began to acquire glass beads from European traders, they adapted their beading skills to use this new type of ornament to decorate clothing and other goods. Today residents of several Mohawk reserves retain these skills, creating floral and geometric beaded designs on a variety of functional and decorative items.

Basketry is another ancient art still cherished by the Mohawk, particularly those living on the Akwesasne Reservation in New York State. Work on a basket begins with the time-consuming task of collecting materials. Akwesasne men first cut black ash trees and then pound the felled trunks to break the wood into strips. Women take the strips and, using handcrafted metal tools, cut and smooth them to produce paper-thin splints. The splints are then soaked to make them pliable. Women also collect and dry sweet grass, which grows wild on the reservation. Interweaving the fragrant sweet grass and the splints produces strong, beautifully textured, and sweet-smelling baskets.

Traditionally, the Mohawk made large, simple baskets in which they stored food. The Akwesasne Mohawk now favor smaller, more ornate basketry. The names of some types—such as sewing and button baskets—indicate their function as small containers. But others are meant to be tiny sculptures that represent for the Mohawk the weaving together of the old and the new.

A rope necklace made from glass beads. Louise McComber, Wolf Clan, Kahnawake Reserve.

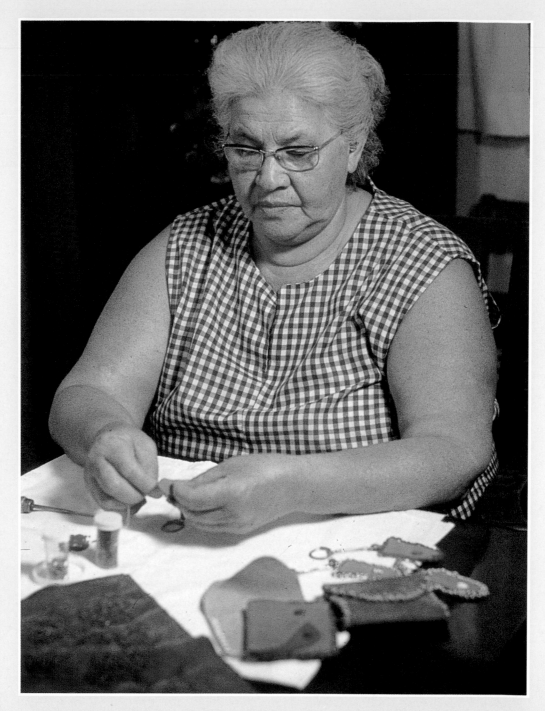

Muriel Nicholas, a member of the Bear Clan, beading at her home on the Oka Reserve.

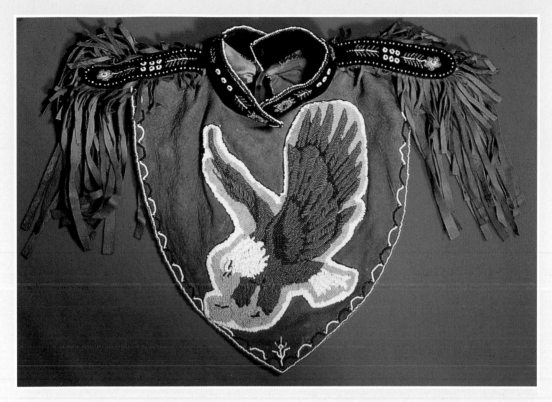

A leather collar adorned with a beaded image of an eagle. Rita Phillips, Wolf Clan, Kahnawake Reserve.

Barrettes made from glass beads and leather. Agnes Decaire, Kahnawake Reserve.

Two cloth whisk-broom holders decorated with floral beadwork designs. Mary Scott Jacobs, Wolf Clan, Kahnawake Reserve.

A glass bead medallion that was woven on a loom. Adeline Etienne, Bear Clan, Oka Reserve.

A bandolier bag made from cloth. The beaded design represents the Celestial Tree, which is described in the Mohawk's creation story. David Maracle, Turtle Clan, Tyendinega Reserve.

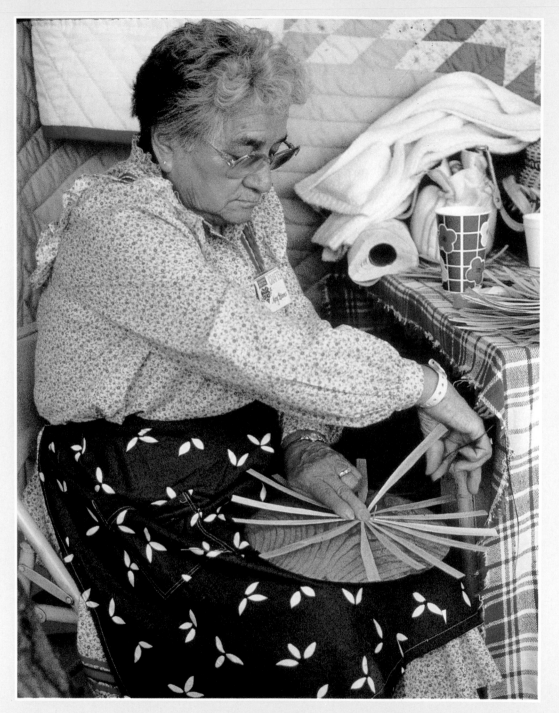

*Mary Adams, a member of the Wolf Clan and resident of the Akwe-
sasne Reservation, has handcrafted baskets for more than 50 years.*

Adams presented this basket to Pope John Paul II in 1980 when 17th-century Mohawk religious figure Kateli Tekak-witha was beatified by the Roman Catholic church.

A lidded basket crafted to commemorate the Strawberry Festival held every June at Akwesasne. Christie Arquette, Turtle Clan, Akwesasne Reservation.

A fancy basket with cover. Cecelia Cree, Wolf Clan, Akwesasne Reservation.

A multicolor fancy basket woven by Mary Adams.

continued from page 56

vert the Mohawk. They rebuilt the chapel at Fort Hunter and opened schools at two Mohawk villages. By 1750, many of the Mohawk in New York were nominally Christian. Along with religious teachings, missionaries encouraged the Indians to trust and support the British. Still, complaints continued about settlers' encroachments upon Mohawk land. In 1753, at a meeting that took place in Albany between Mohawk leaders and Governor Clinton, the Mohawk chief Hendrick spoke bitterly of the colonists' occupation of Indian land. He carefully detailed case after case of illegalities:

> Barclay, Pitchetts wife. We let her have a little spot of land and she takes in more and more every year.

> We have a complaint against Arent Stevens. He bought a tract of land of us, and when the surveyor came to survey it, we showed him how far to go, and then Arent Stevens came and told him he had employed him and made him go a great deal further.

> We have another complaint against Conradt Gunterman. We gave him a tract of land out of charity but he takes in more which we have not given or sold him.

> Johannes Lawyers Patent at Stonerabie to no further than the Creek. He has taken up six miles further than the Creek.

> Honnes Clock claims an island below the Indian Castle at Conojohary which was never sold to any person.

Although Clinton tried to reassure Hendrick that Mohawk accusations would be properly investigated, Hendrick replied that the "covenant chain of friendship" between his nation and Great Britain was broken. Alarmed by the possibility of losing Iroquois allegiance, the government in London ordered a full accounting of land deals and protection of Indian rights. However, as in the past, colonial administrators were ineffective. They rarely came to the aid of the Indians; instead, they turned a blind eye to settlers' abuses.

One particularly serious complaint involved a huge tract of 800,000 acres of land north of the Mohawk River and west of the Hudson River. The attorney general of New York, Sampson Broughton, said that he had purchased this land from the Mohawk Nation in 1703 for 60 pounds (about $150). The Indians asserted that Broughton's claim was false. They declared that the area he claimed was too large, that no money had ever been paid, and that the transaction was invalid in any case because only two of the three Mohawk clans had agreed to the sale. Although the Mohawk repeatedly sought redress in this case, it was not until 1768 that the government completed an investigation. An agreement was finally reached in which the Mohawk consented to sell the eastern portion of the original tract for $5,000. They retained a smaller section to the west.

As more settlers moved into the Mohawk Valley, trading posts expanded their operations, relying on both native and immigrant commerce. Posts were built all along the Mohawk River and even farther west as an increased British military presence made colonists and merchants feel secure. Although many Mohawk prospered from trade, their anger over unscrupulous land transactions made them wary of long-term British intentions.

Despite their misgivings, the Mohawk fulfilled pledges of aid for Great Britain's cause during the French and Indian War of 1755–62. This conflict would be the final major battle between England and France for control of what is now the eastern United States. Many Mohawk warriors fought and died helping the British. Chief Hendrick was among the casualties, dying at the Battle of Lake George in 1755. The war ended with a British victory. In the peace agreement between the two European adversaries, Indian rights to their lands were recognized. In spite of British pledges, the 40,000 acres originally granted to the Mohawk at Kahnawake near Montreal were immediately reduced by half.

After the end of the war, France was forced to withdraw its armies from the Northeast, which left the Iroquois looking forward to a lasting peace. But even though the Mohawk had fought as loyal allies of Great Britain, they did not receive the rewards of victory. As settlers arrived in ever-increasing numbers and occupied Indian territory, the Mohawk

tried to keep what little land they had left.

At this time, the English government also began doubting its own security in North America. Colonial rebelliousness alarmed English officials. They realized that if the Iroquois were not satisfied with British protection, the Indians might turn against the Crown as well. Britain was therefore forced to listen to Iroquois complaints. They negotiated a treaty at Fort Stanwix in 1768 that established definite boundaries between Indian and British territory.

Some colonial officials also recognized the injustices that had been committed against the Indians and seriously attempted to make amends. Among these was Sir William Johnson, who had formerly been a trader to the Mohawk and had served as a superintendent of Indian affairs for New York. He often spoke on the Mohawk's behalf, intervening in conflicts between Indians and settlers. However, the gap between individual intentions and government actions was as wide as ever.

By the 1770s, many colonists were indeed rebelling against British authority. The rebels recognized the role that the Iroquois could play in helping or hindering their cause. In 1775, Iroquois leaders were invited to Albany for a meeting with the rebels—or Americans—led by Philip Schuyler. At that time, the Americans believed that the best they could hope for was Iroquoian neutrality. The Mohawk at the meeting raised issues of land claims against col-

John Verelst's painting of Tee Yee Neen Ho Ga Row, who was called Hendrick by the British. Hendrick died in 1755 while battling French troops in the French and Indian War.

onists. After the rebels gave words of assurance, the Iroquois pledged to be neutral if the colonists did indeed revolt. In return, the Americans promised to give the Indians a store of supplies, especially warm clothing.

The Continental Congress—the legislature established in 1774 by the revolting colonists—also tried to secure the friendship of Iroquois leaders. In the summer of 1775, Congress sent a message to the confederacy:

> In our consultation we have judged it proper and necessary to send you this talk, as we are upon the same island, that you may be informed of the reasons of this great Council. . . .
> This is a family quarrel between us and old England. We desire you to remain at home, and not join on either side, but keep the hatchet buried deep.

For their part, the British attempted to use their long-standing alliance with the Iroquois to convince Indians to fight against the revolutionaries. In July 1775, Sir Frederick Haldimand, governor of Canada, met with Mohawk leaders and told them:

> Now is the time for you to help the King. The war has begun. Assist the King now, and you will find it to your advantage. Go now and fight for your possessions, and whatever you lose of your property during the war, the King will make up to you when peace returns.

An ornament owned by Joseph Brant. The design was derived from an insignia worn by British military officers.

Because the British were well aware of the Iroquois' need of European goods, they tried to become their sole suppliers of clothing and other necessities so that the Indians would remain loyal to them. In 1776, they successfully cut off the flow of American goods when they defeated American troops led by George Washington in New York City.

British officials also used their friendship with several influential Mohawk leaders to enlist Indian support. Joseph Brant, grandson of one of the

Four Indian Kings entertained in London in 1710 and himself a powerful leader and orator, was invited to England. There he heard numerous arguments favoring Iroquois military assistance for Great Britain. Brant returned to New York and spoke vigorously in support of the British cause at council meetings of the confederacy. The league refused to endorse officially either the British or American side. Three nations—the Mohawk, the Seneca, and the Cayuga—favored the British. The Oneida and Tuscarora leaned toward the Americans, and the Onondaga, divided among themselves, were unable to take a stand. Without a consensus, the Iroquois Confederacy adopted a position of neutrality, more by default than by conviction. The dissension among its members shook the stability of the league because the confederacy had always drawn its strength from the principle of unanimity, of One Heart, One Mind, One Law. Reacting to insurmountable disagreements among the nations, confederacy leaders covered up the council fire at the principal Onondaga village in 1777. This symbolic gesture foreshadowed the end of the league as a dominant political and military force in the region.

Many Mohawk leaders and warriors remained neutral during the Revolution. Others, led by Joseph Brant, supported the British. Several considerations led to their decision. First, after 1776, the British had succeeded in becoming the Mohawk's greatest supplier of tools, clothing, and weapons. The Indians' economic dependence was translated into a military alliance. Second, the Mohawk continued to be wary of colonists' incursions into their territory. They were warned by British officials that a rebel victory would signal the end of the Indians' control over their land. The British argued that the rebels could not be trusted to respect the Mohawk's land claims. Their prediction was supported by an action of the New York legislature during the Revolution. The state claimed all Indian land within its boundaries and promised to give 600 acres to anyone who enlisted in the rebel army.

Some Mohawk were persuaded to continue their military alliance with Great Britain, and others fought on the side of the Americans. Most, though, remained neutral. Regardless of their allegiances, Mohawk communities around Albany were targets of retaliation by American settlers. Crops were burned, livestock was stolen, and people were attacked. In 1779, an American army under General John Sullivan destroyed Iroquois villages throughout New York.

The Treaty of Paris in 1783 formally concluded the revolutionary war. It also marked the end of what little security the Mohawk had had in New York. The treaty transferred British territory as far west as the Mississippi River to the victorious Americans. It was, however, absolutely silent on the issue of Indian rights to land in this area. Only the governor of Canada, Sir Frederick Haldimand, spoke up for Indian claims at the

A letter from Joseph Brant to a British official in which the Mohawk leader requested supplies for his people. The Mohawk's reliance on English goods was one of the major reasons they chose to support the British during the revolutionary war.

treaty conference. He argued that the natives did not think Great Britain had the right to cede their lands to the United States and wanted to maintain the boundaries provided in the 1768 Treaty of Fort Stanwix. Haldimand's recommendations were ignored. By the early 1780s, most of the Mohawk had left their traditional lands in New York to seek safety in Canada.

The Mohawk refugees slowly began the process of rebuilding their lives in Canada, hoping finally to live and prosper in peace. They came to reside in five communities—each of which had its own complex history and unique problems and opportunities. The people hoped to be able to reaffirm the ancestral bonds that had kept them of One Mind for so many centuries. But these bonds had been torn asunder by conflicts that the Mohawk did not create but that had, in the end, engulfed them nonetheless. ▲

A group of Akwesasne Mohawk in 1894 in Lawrence, Kansas. The Indians traveled to Lawrence to sell baskets in markets there.

A NATION
DIVIDED

Most of the Mohawk had emigrated from their traditional lands by the end of the 18th century and settled in several communities where they hoped to reestablish their lives in tranquillity and harmony. The first Mohawk refugees in the 17th century wanted to escape from intertribal conflicts caused by economic competition over the fur trade. A hundred years later, those who had founded settlements left their aboriginal territory because of warfare between Great Britain and the American colonies. In all cases, the Mohawk had to adjust to new circumstances beyond their control. They did so while trying to maintain as much of their traditional culture as possible.

Founded in 1667, the mission settlement of Kahnawake, La Prairie, was located south of Montreal on land granted by the king of France and owned in trust by the Jesuits. Although the majority of Kahnawake's residents were Mohawk, members of other nations in the Iroquois Confederacy sought refuge there as well.

As Kahnawake grew, it became famous for several of its inhabitants. These included a chief known both as Kryn and as Joseph Togouiroui (to-go-wee-RO-wee), who had led a group of 40 Catholic Mohawks from New York to Kahnawake in 1673. Another illustrious 17th-century resident was a devout woman named Kateli Tekakwitha (ga-de-LEE de-ga-GWEE-ta). Her piety and good works were admired by many of her contemporaries. In recognition of her devotion, Tekakwitha has recently become the first American Indian to be declared by the Catholic church as venerable and beatified, two steps toward possible sainthood.

The Jesuit missionaries were enthusiastic about the progress of converts at Kahnawake, noting their piety and moral character. In the words of one priest, Father Claude Chauchetiéré, writing in 1694:

> Anger is the chief one of their passions, but they are not carried away to excess by it, even in war. Living in common, without disputes, content with little, guiltless of avarice, and assiduous at work, it is impossible to find a people more patient, more hospitable, more affable, more liberal, more moderate in their language.

The community at Kahnawake shifted residence several times in the 17th and 18th centuries. These moves were necessary because of the depletion of nearby soil, making it unsuitable for planting corn. Kahnawake's present location was established in 1716 on the southern shore of the St. Lawrence River, across from Montreal. The settlement continued to grow. By 1736, an estimated 300 families resided there.

Living only a few miles from the growing city of Montreal, Kahnawake's inhabitants were under considerable pressure to adopt Canadian mores. Missionaries urged these Mohawk to conform to European standards. The priests instructed married couples to remain together, condemned sexual activity before or outside of marriage, and criticized Mohawk curing practices.

Harmful influences from French settlements sometimes reached Kahnawake. In 1735, Father Luc-Francois Nau commented:

> The Iroquois are more inclined to the practice of virtue than other nations; they are capable of refined feelings but the bad example and solicitations of the French are a very great obstacle to the sanctification of our Iroquois. . . . Taking all into consideration, our Iroquois are much better Christians than the French.

For nearly 100 years after its founding, the people at Kahnawake often had to choose between allegiance to their kin in New York or to their non-Indian protectors in Quebec. They tried to remain neutral but were continually besieged with requests for aid by both sides. Because of the daily influence of French Jesuits at Kahnawake, the Mohawk there more frequently allied themselves with the French than with their former neighbors. The Kahnawake Mohawk regretted the breach between them and their relatives remaining in New York. French observer Pierre Charlevoix commented that in leaving their ancestral territory, the Mohawk had "abandoned everything that was dearest to them." He added that this was "a sacrifice still more glorious for Indians than for any other nation, because there are none so much attached as they are to their families and their native country."

During the 18th century, the Kahnawake Mohawk engaged in the traditional economic tasks of farming, hunting, and fishing. Women planted

French Jesuit Pierre Charlevoix visited the Kahnawake Mohawk in the early 18th century.

and harvested their crops. Men left their village for extended periods in autumn and winter to hunt deer and beaver. In addition, the Mohawk raised livestock—such as pigs, poultry, and horses—that had been introduced to North America by Europeans. At Kahnawake, large matrilineal families also lived together in longhouses built in the Iroquoian style. The three Mohawk clans—Bear, Wolf, and Turtle—added to their membership by adopting newcomers from other Indian groups.

Toward the end of the 18th century, the fur trade declined in the Northeast because of dwindling supplies of animals. A number of Mohawk men from Kahnawake and Akwesasne then obtained employment as trappers, loggers, and canoeists with the North West Company, a large fur-trading concern. They headed west across Canada and established a settlement of approximately 250 people in Alberta. Many of these Mohawk remained in Alberta and married into local Indian communities, especially those of the Cree. They were given 25,600 acres of land in Alberta by the Canadian government. (The tract was later reduced to 15,485 acres.) In the 1940s, these lands were expropriated by the province of Alberta. Although their territory was taken away, descendants of this Mohawk group still live in Alberta, British Columbia, and Montana.

In the 19th century, men at Kahnawake gradually abandoned hunting. They had less access to forests because of the expansion of Canadian settlements. Farming gained in importance, providing food for residents and produce for sale to neighboring communities. In addition, Mohawk women received income from the sale of handicrafts, such as basketry and beadwork embroidery.

The legal status of Kahnawake as a mission settlement changed in 1830. The community was reconstituted as a reserve, the Canadian equivalent of a reservation in the United States. As a reserve, the land would be held in common by all of its Indian residents and would not be taxed by the Canadian

A classroom of Mohawk students at Kahnawake in the 1930s.

government. As soon as the reserve was established, the Canadian government began to interfere with Mohawk custom by allotting individual homesteads to each male head of a household. The traditional composition of Mohawk households, which had always been headed by women, was broken up in an effort to impose the way of life of non-Indian Canadians on the residents of Kahnawake.

The Mohawk mission village of Kanesatake had been built in 1676 on land granted to the Mohawk by Sulpician missionaries on the island of Montreal. After several moves, a permanent settlement was established in 1721 at Lake-of-Two-Mountains, a short distance west of Montreal. The community at Kanesatake, meaning "place of reeds" or "at the foot of the hillside," is sometimes referred to by its Algonkian name Oka (walleyed pike).

In the 1880s, a group of people left Kanesatake and established a small reserve called Wahta (WAH-da), meaning "maple," near Parry Sound, southeast of Georgian Bay in Ontario. This settlement, also called Gibson Reserve, had approximately 250 residents in the 19th century.

Sometime between 1747 and 1755, a third settlement of Catholic Mohawk was founded along the St. Lawrence approximately 80 miles southwest of Montreal. This community—known both as Akwesasne (ah-gwe-SAS-ne), meaning "where the partridge drums," and as St. Regis—was established by people from Kahnawake who had left in search of better soil. The population had grown at Kahnawake, creating a shortage of land and thereby adding another incentive for these people to emigrate. French authorities in Montreal encouraged the new settlement at Akwesasne because they wanted to have another outpost along the St. Lawrence.

Later, during the American Revolution, the inhabitants of Akwesasne divided into pro-British and pro-American factions. Although most sided with the British, many fought in support of the rebels. A Mohawk leader named Louis Cook (also known as Colonel Louis) was acknowledged by George Washington for his efforts on the Americans' behalf. Washington wrote from Cambridge, Massachusetts, to the Continental Congress in January 1776:

> On Sunday evening, thirteen of the [Mohawk] Indians arrived here on a visit. I shall take care that they be so entertained during their stay, that they may return impressed with sentiments of friendship for us, and also of our great strength. One of them is Colonel Louis, who honored me with a visit once before.

After the war, the Treaty of Paris set the boundary between Canada and the United States at 45 degrees north latitude. This line arbitrarily divided Akwesasne into Canadian and American sections. In 1791, New York State sold a large tract of Akwesasne territory to a New Yorker named Alexander Macomb. An area of only six miles square and two islands in the St. Lawrence were reserved for the Mohawk. They immediately petitioned the state government in Albany, asserting claims to more land. An agreement was finally reached in 1796 that granted the Akwesasne Mohawk two additional tracts of one mile square each along two small rivers. Other portions of their land were sold by New York State in the first half of the 19th century, leaving them with 14,000 acres in New York State and 10,000 acres in Canada. In exchange for these cessions, yearly payments, or annuities, were also guaranteed to the Akwesasne Mohawk.

In the early 19th century, the Akwesasne Mohawk were affected by another external war. During the War of 1812 between Great Britain and the United States, authorities in New York prohibited people from Akwesasne to travel outside the reserve unless they secured official passes. This restriction

severely limited men's ability to hunt.
Even worse, residents were unable to
obtain clothing, tools, or other necessary provisions. Indian leaders reacted
by requesting supplies from the government. In a letter to Albany, Louis
Cook wrote:

> I address you these lines, for the
> purpose of expressing the situation of
> my nation, and of giving you
> assurances of our constantly
> cherishing good will and friendship
> towards the United States, and of our
> determination not to intermeddle with
> the war which has broken out
> between them and the English, and
> which has placed us in so critical a
> situation. Our young men being
> prevented from hunting, and
> obtaining a subsistence for their
> families, are in want of provisions,
> and I address myself in their behalf to
> the justice and liberality of the
> governor of this state, to obtain a
> supply of beef, pork and flour, to be
> delivered to us at St. Regis, during
> the time that we are compelled to
> give up our accustomed pursuits.

Cook's request was granted.

Both the British and American governments agreed that Akwesasne
should remain neutral in the conflict.
However, Akwesasne residents became involved on both sides during the
war. Cook joined American forces, as
he had during the American Revolution. He was captured by British soldiers in a battle at St. Regis in 1813 and
taken to a prison in Quebec, where he
died the following year.

After the War of 1812, Canada and
the United States began to enforce border restrictions. Before that time, the
Akwesasne Mohawk had held their
land in common, ignoring the international border. After the war, officials in
New York started to issue annuities
only to those Indians living on the
American side. Canadian authorities
barred the New York Mohawk from
taking up residence in Canada.

The community was governed locally by two sets of leaders. On the Ca-

The Mohawk community of Akwesasne, depicted in an engraving by W. B. Bartlett from about 1850.

nadian side, 12 chiefs, selected for life terms, formed an administrative council. These chiefs were chosen from kinship groups in accordance with traditional customs. In New York, a council of three trustees, serving three-year terms, carried out government functions.

People at Akwesasne suffered throughout the 19th century from epidemic diseases, especially outbreaks of smallpox, cholera, and typhus. In response to these health crises, New York State opened clinics at Akwesasne in the late 19th century. It also gave financial relief, food, and clothing to poor people. Then, in the early 20th century, New York authorities began an investigation of living conditions on all reservations within the state. Officials undertook this review for two reasons: Medical experts feared that a smallpox epidemic occurring in the Seneca reservations in western New York would spread to neighboring communities. In addition, the state was embroiled in legal battles over Indian land claims. Edward Everett, a state legislator from St. Lawrence County, near the Akwesasne reservation, was appointed in 1919 to head a commission of inquiry. Everett's panel heard testimony by residents of Iroquois reservations in New York and Canada. In order to determine the legal history of Indian claims, the commissioners reviewed the treaties that the Iroquois had concluded with the United States. Everett based his final report on the 1784 Treaty of Fort Stanwix in which the federal government transferred title to lands occupied by Indians in New York State to the Indians themselves, including the Akwesasne Mohawk. Everett declared:

> The passing of the title for this ceded territory to the Indians of this state was a legal and proper transaction. And the Indians, as a nation, became possessed of the ceded territory.

Finally, Everett concluded:

> The said Indians of the State of New York, as a nation, are still the owners of the fee simple title to the territory ceded to them by the Treaty of 1784, unless divested of the same by an instrument of equal force and effect as the said treaty of 1784.

In all, Everett declared that New York Iroquois were still owners of 6 million acres of land in New York State. State authorities predictably objected to his conclusions. They refused to consider seriously the facts he presented or to recognize Indian rights. Officials reacted by trying to broaden their control over reservation communities. For instance, in the 1950s, the state extended its jurisdiction over Indian lands in criminal and civil matters.

Within 30 years after the founding of Akwesasne in the 18th century, a fourth Mohawk community was established in Canada. The community was settled in 1777 by a group of Mohawk led by Captain John Deserontyon, who had supported the British before and during the American Revolution. The village was located on the north shore of the Bay of Quinté on the northeastern waterways of Lake Ontario. The community was known both as Tyendinega (ti-yen-di-NE-ga), the Mohawk name of Joseph Brant, and as Deseranto, after its founder. Locally, it was administered by a council of 11 hereditary chiefs chosen for life from the 11 matrilineal groups that first settled there.

Many other Mohawk took up residence in a fifth community in Canada, founded just after the end of the American Revolution. This settlement is called Six Nations because its inhabitants were members of all the nations of the Iroquois Confederacy. Six Nations' original residents were either neutral or

MOHAWK RESERVES AND RESERVATIONS

QUEBEC

Ottawa   *River*

ONTARIO

OKA RESERVE △

● **Montreal**

Ottawa ★

ST. REGIS RESERVE △

CAUGHNAWAGA RESERVE

ST. REGIS RESERVATION

GIBSON RESERVE △

St. Lawrence River

TYENDINEGA RESERVE △

Toronto ●

LAKE   ONTARIO

● **Oswego**

Rochester ●

SIX NATIONS RESERVE △

NEW YORK

Schenectady ●

LAKE   ERIE

Buffalo ●

● **Albany**

CANADA   area of map

UNITED STATES

British-allied Iroquois who sought refuge from American attacks and retaliations taking place in New York. They were led by Joseph Brant, who had always remained loyal to Great Britain.

In 1784, these Indians founded their new community along the Grand River in southern Ontario, a short distance from the American border. The land had been purchased for the Mohawk and their allies by Sir Frederick Haldimand, governor of Canada, from a group of Indians called the Mississaugas. Haldimand was fulfilling a pledge he made during the war to compensate Indians who fought for England for any losses they suffered as a result of their loyalty. The tract encompassed 6 miles of land along both sides of the river, totaling 675,000 acres. The population of Six Nations in 1785 consisted of 1,600 Iroquois, including 450 Mohawks, 380 Cayugas, 200 Onondagas, 165 Oneidas, 125 Tuscaroras, and 75 Senecas.

Members of each nation set up a separate village. Like other groups of displaced Mohawk, the people at Six Nations tried to reestablish their culture even though their world had changed forever. As a symbol of determination to assert Iroquois identities and traditions, clan chiefs rekindled the confederacy fire at the Onondaga village at Six Nations. Local government was managed by a council composed of hereditary chiefs from all the nations. Although the six nations were considered equals, Mohawk prominence in the community was evident in that all chiefs spoke the Mohawk language in council deliberations.

Joseph Brant had considerable influence on politics at Six Nations. He believed that the Iroquois should remain strong and sovereign in their new home. He also thought that they needed to adopt some practices of Canadian and American society in order to be economically self-sufficient. Brant urged leaders to sell a large portion of land to Canadian farmers because he hoped that the success of these people would be a good example for the Iroquois. In addition, he wanted to use money received for land to buy food and clothing for indigent Iroquois until they could provide for themselves. After years of debate, some 350,000 acres of land were sold to Canadians, many of whom were friends of Brant's.

Most Iroquois had small farms on which women planted traditional crops using aboriginal farming methods. A few people were able to amass larger holdings. They adopted farming methods introduced by Canadians and grew new crops, such as oats, wheat, and peas. Significantly, these farmers were men, reflecting a shift from the tradition of women being responsible for all farm work.

Throughout the first half of the 19th century, farm production gradually increased until many families at Six Nations were fairly prosperous. They produced surpluses, which they sold at markets in nearby cities, such as Brantford and Hamilton in Ontario.

Influences from Canadian society also intensified. Protestant missionaries first built churches at Six Nations in 1827. The Mohawk Institute, a school for Iroquois children, opened in Brantford at about the same time. The first school at Six Nations was constructed in 1831 by Anglican missionaries. Located in the Mohawk community, it offered formal education to all children. In addition, teachers instructed girls in domestic skills and boys in farming techniques. At first, people showed little interest in the schools, but gradually more students were enrolled. Missionaries continued to control education at Six Nations until the late 1800s. Many people opposed the schools because they were afraid that exposure to Canadian education would lead to increased assimilation and eventual loss of independence. In response to these

Mohawk men photographed while building a bridge in the late 19th century. At this time, the Mohawk increasingly came to rely on wage work for their livelihood.

fears, the Mohawk worked to establish Indian-run schools, and by 1880, 13 schools were operating.

The people at Six Nations experienced serious health problems in the 19th century. They suffered especially from smallpox, measles, and cholera. After a number of years of intermittent medical care, a permanent doctor was employed in 1850 to serve the residents. In 1900, the Six Nations Council established a Board of Health to encourage and coordinate provision of medical services. A tent hospital was opened in 1908. It was replaced in 1927 by the Lady Willingdon Hospital, named after the wife of the Marquess of Willingdon, Governor-general of Canada from 1926 to 1931.

As in other Iroquois communities, internal and external pressures to sell additional land continued at Six Nations. Many Indians opposed such sales because they feared losing all their land and their culture. In 1841, the council agreed to turn over Six Nations' land to the British crown to be held in trust. The Canadian government assumed responsibility for evicting non-Indian squatters who had illegally moved onto portions of Six Nations' territory. In the following year, the community was legally formed as a reserve for the Iroquois. Since then, land could only be sold if a majority of the people expressed their approval in a referendum.

Shortly after the reserve was established, the Canadian government began a program of dividing lands into small plots, called allotments, that would be owned by individuals. The aim of allotting the reserve was to compel the Iroquois to give up the custom of communal land ownership, which non-Indians saw as an obstacle to the Indians' assimilation into mainstream Canadian society. Between 1847 and 1848, each male head of a household was given an allotment of 100 acres. By 1848, 325 families, consisting of 1,271 individuals, had complied with the program.

The government's policies had far-reaching consequences for Iroquoian culture: First, stressing individual rather than communal ownership of land eroded the Iroquois' unity. Second, land was allotted only to nuclear families—groups made up of a man, a woman, and their children—resulting in the breakup of large extended families that had traditionally been the basis of economic cooperation and interdependence. And third, the program assigned land to men, undermining the roles and rights of women as producers and controllers of food. Not surprisingly, many women resisted the changes because they recognized the danger to their own status. As they feared, women were pressured into giving up productive and public roles in the community. Instead, they became isolated in separate households dominated by their fathers and husbands.

Throughout the second half of the 19th century, farming continued to gain importance as a source of food and income from the sale of surpluses. In 1867, the Mohawk founded the Six Nations Agricultural Society, which disseminated technological innovations to the community. It also sponsored annual fairs to showcase the accomplishments of local farmers.

By the early years of the 20th century, the role of agriculture at Six Nations had declined. Small farms were gradually abandoned because they were no longer financially profitable. However, several large farms were quite prosperous. These farms produced various kinds of grains, including corn, oats, and wheat. People also kept livestock, such as dairy and beef cattle, poultry, hogs, and sheep. They sold surplus produce, milk, and animals in nearby Canadian cities.

Unfortunately, these businesses soon began to face financial difficulties. The 1930s—the years of the Great Depression—were especially hard. In order to continue to produce surpluses, Six Nations farmers realized that they needed money to invest in new equipment. But Indians living on reserves had problems obtaining bank loans. Their land was held in trust by the band (the Canadian word for tribe) and therefore could not be used as collateral for a loan. Since the Great Depression, farming has contributed less and less to tribal incomes.

By the late 19th century, Mohawk men not engaged in farming were employed in a variety of occupations. They worked at Six Nations or nearby towns and cities as blacksmiths, carpenters, builders, and factory laborers.

During this period, conflicts arose over the local form of government. The hereditary chiefs who formed the councils tended to be traditionalists. They spoke their native language and opposed the rapid assimilation of Canadian practices. Some were Christians; others followed the traditional religion. These differences often caused rifts within their ranks and made consensus difficult. As a result, some Mohawk Indians began to petition for a change in government. Instead of leadership by hereditary chiefs, they wanted to establish a council of elected representatives. This group called itself the Dehorners, after the traditional method of "dehorning" or impeaching clan chiefs. The Dehorners thought that an elected council would be less divided and more responsive to the people. Others at Six Nations preferred to keep the traditional council. They supported the Iroquois Confederacy and argued that hereditary chiefs symbolized the continuity and sovereignty of the league.

For many years, Canadian authorities refused to mediate the dispute. Then, in 1924, the Canadian Parliament unilaterally dissolved the hereditary system of leadership. The Canadian government wanted to establish an elective system at Six Nations because it believed that such a government would help "modernize" the reserve. The government also knew that hereditary leaders were more likely to fight

to hold on to their lands and traditional cultural practices. It called for elections beginning in October 1924.

During the Six Nations Council meeting that September, one month before elections, officers of the Royal Canadian Mounted Police locked the doors to the council chamber during a lunch break while hereditary leaders were absent. The chiefs were thus unable to return to the council hall. Many people, both supporters and opponents of the traditional system, were angered by this display of force. But the elections were held as scheduled. Six electoral districts were set up, each choosing two representatives. In this council of 12 members, each official served for a 2-year term. At first, only men could vote in reserve elections. Suffrage was finally extended to women in 1951.

Most residents of the three original mission settlements of Kahnawake, Kanesatake, and Akwesasne were Catholic. Tyendinega and Six Nations were founded by people who followed either the traditional Mohawk religion or various Protestant faiths. However, shortly after these 2 communities were established in the late 18th century, a new religion was introduced on a Sen-

A meeting of the chiefs of the Iroquois Confederacy in 1910. Hanging on the wall is a British flag, banners decorated with clan symbols, and framed portraits of Mohawk and European leaders.

Jesse Cornplanter's 1903 illustration of the Spirit of Corn speaking to Handsome Lake, the 18th-century Seneca prophet.

eca reservation in New York. In 1799, a Seneca man named Handsome Lake became deathly ill after years of sickness. During his illness, he received a vision from supernatural messengers instructing him to preach a new faith, or the Good Word, among his people. He recovered and proceeded to make known the message he had received. Known today as the Handsome Lake Religion or the Longhouse Religion, the Good Word advises people to return to traditional Iroquoian ethics of cooperation, generosity, and kindness. Many aspects of traditional culture were reinforced by Handsome Lake, including the Four Sacred Rituals and the annual cycle of calendric ceremonies.

Handsome Lake also stressed the importance of sobriety. His statements against alcohol greatly contributed to his popularity and influence. Handsome Lake was responsible for strengthening the temperance movement not only among the Seneca, Cayuga, and Tuscarora but also among non-Indians in western New York State.

The religious leader encouraged his people to adopt some Canadian and American practices as well. Among these were non-Indian gender roles and relationships. Handsome Lake favored organizing households of nuclear rather than extended families. He also advocated weakening the bonds between mothers and daughters and strengthening male authority in marital relationships. In addition, he encouraged the use of non-Indian farming methods, especially making farm work the responsibility of men.

Handsome Lake opposed beliefs and practices related to witchcraft. In fact, accusations of witchcraft were often made against prominent women who resisted attempts to curtail their economic and political activities.

The Handsome Lake Religion spread rapidly, first among the Seneca reservations in New York and then to Six Nations in Canada. By the middle of the 19th century, followers of Handsome Lake constituted approximately 20 to 25 percent of the Six Nations population, a ratio that remains essentially constant today. The Longhouse Religion was adopted by the Mohawk at Kahnawake in the 1920s and at Akwesasne in the 1930s. Its adherents at both of these reserves constituted a smaller percentage of the population than at Six Nations, but they had great influence on social and political activities.

By the middle of the 20th century, the people of the various Mohawk communities were adapting to somewhat different local conditions. However, there were also many similarities in their circumstances. All Mohawk had felt pressure to sell lands that had been guaranteed to them forever. Mohawk people from every community often lost out to Canadian and American encroachments but managed to hold on to enough land to assure their survival. They also experienced pressure to assimilate aspects of non-Indian culture. Traditional household groups were disbanded, economic roles were realigned, and native religious beliefs were modified or replaced. But the Mohawk shared much more than these experiences. They were still drawn together by their past and the enduring traditions of the confederacy. ▲

Thomas Grey, one of the many residents of the Akwesasne Reserve who make their living by crafting and selling traditional baskets.

6

THE "REAL PEOPLE" TODAY

In the Mohawk language, the word for Native American is *onkwehonwe* (on-gwe-HON-we), or "real people." Since their first contact with Europeans, the real people have struggled against countless attacks and injustices. All across North America, they have seen their lands diminished, their rights restricted, and their cultures transformed. Many Indian societies were not able to withstand the physical onslaught of foreign armies or the pressure to adapt to foreign cultural practices. But many other Indian peoples have survived and maintained their distinctive values and ways of life. Among these are the Mohawk. Drawing on their past history, the Mohawk in the 20th century have adapted to external conditions, creating their own definition of their place in the modern world.

All Mohawk communities have experienced economic, political, and so-cial changes. Wage work has become the mainstay of Mohawk families. At Six Nations, men and women are employed in businesses and factories in nearby towns and cities. Some men work as mechanics, miners, and builders. Others are employed in automobile factories in Buffalo, New York, and Oakville, Ontario. Women often have jobs as nurses, teachers, factory workers, or service employees.

Many men of Akwesasne and Kahnawake are employed as ironworkers in the construction of bridges and buildings. The Mohawk first became involved in this industry in 1886, when the Dominion Bridge Company negotiated with the Kahnawake Council for access to land through which the firm wished to build a railroad bridge that would stretch across the St. Lawrence River from Montreal to the Quebec mainland near the reserve. In exchange for the use of some reserve land, the company agreed to hire Kahnawake men. After the bridge was completed, many Kahnawake workers helped build the international Soo Bridge that connects Sault Ste. Marie, Ontario, and Sault Ste. Marie, Michigan. Since then, the Mohawk have been attracted to this occupation in large numbers. They have erected bridges and skyscrapers throughout the Northeast. In fact, most Akwesasne and Kahnawake men are employed in high-steel construction for at least some period of their life. These men work in numerous cities, including Buffalo, Rochester, Syracuse, New York, and Boston. They obviously cannot commute to and from their homes and work sites daily, so they reside in city apartments during the week and return to their reserves on the weekend. These men have formed close groups that travel, work, and live together.

Although Mohawk ironworkers usually maintain homes at either Kahnawake or Akwesasne, many families establish residences in cities where the men work. For instance, a sizable Mohawk community grew up in New York City's borough of Brooklyn. During the 1960s and 1970s—the peak years of construction in New York—this community numbered nearly 1,000. As a result of the decline in the availability of work in the 1980s and 1990s, most Mohawk families have returned to Kahnawake and Akwesasne. Only about 100 Mohawks continue to maintain permanent residences in the city.

Because of Kahnawake's location near Montreal, it is one of the most urbanized reserves in Canada. Many people work in Montreal and other Canadian towns and cities close to the reserve. Although Akwesasne is not as urban as Kahnawake, men and women there also work in a wide variety of professional and skilled occupations in nearby Canadian and American locations. The people at Kahnawake and Akwesasne have the highest income per capita of any Canadian reserve.

At the three largest Mohawk reserves—Six Nations, Kahnawake, and Akwesasne—income is generated by employment in band offices, schools, restaurants, stores, and gas stations. Each of these reserves has at least one central village where offices, schools, and stores are located. Ohsweken at Six Nations has a council house, community hall, hospital, police headquarters, post office, and several schools and churches. At Akwesasne, administrative, cultural, and business establishments are located at St. Regis Village in Quebec and at the Community Center, a complex of public buildings near Hogansburg in New York. The village at Kahnawake has band offices, stores, and a hospital.

People living on the three smallest Mohawk reserves—Kanesatake, Tyendinega, and Gibson—have fewer opportunities for employment in their own communities. Some residents of Gibson own cranberry farms on which they produce 10 to 25 percent of Canada's supply of this fruit. Most mem-

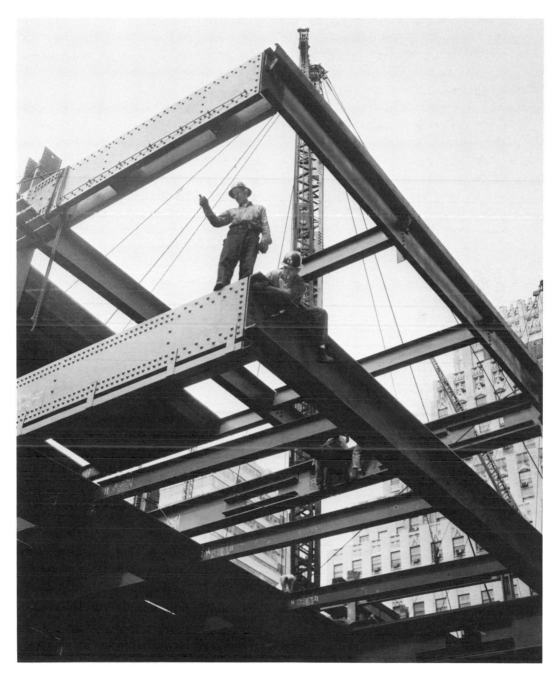

Mohawk steelworkers on the girders of a Manhattan skyscraper. In the late 20th century, many Mohawk men have found jobs in construction.

bers of these three reserves obtain jobs on nearby farms or in factories and other businesses. For people at all Mohawk reserves, income derived from off-reserve employment is, on average, about 150 percent greater than that obtained from on-reserve work.

In some Mohawk communities, disagreements have grown over questions of leadership and political direction. Governing councils on all the reserves are now chosen through elections. However, this system encounters a number of problems. Popular involvement in elections is actually quite low. The contests are usually decided by less than one-third of the eligible voters.

The low voter turnout may be caused, in part, by apathy. More significant, though, is many people's opposition to an elective system. Instead of holding elections, they want to reestablish leadership by hereditary chiefs.

Opposition to elective government is often well organized. At Six Nations, many traditionalists have actively sought a change in the system. In 1959, a group of hereditary chiefs, with the help of 1,300 supporters, tried to oust the elected council and reinstate themselves as the reserves' official leaders. On March 5, they took over the band council offices, proclaiming the end of the elective system. The chiefs and their

Mohawk from the Caughnawaga Reserve protesting against the policies of the Canadian government in 1964.

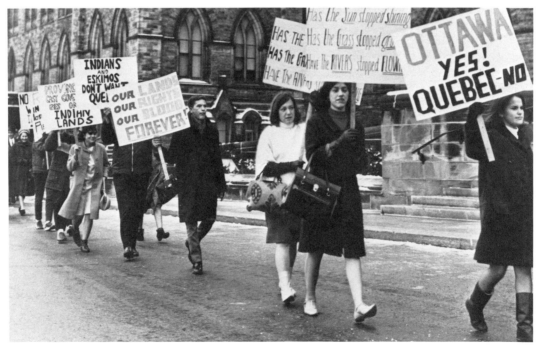

followers occupied the council house for one week before being evicted by the Royal Canadian Mounted Police. Even though the occupation ended, dissatisfaction with the elective system continues.

At Kahnawake and Akwesasne, hereditary chiefs are respected members of their communities. Although they do not hold elected office, these leaders wield considerable social and political influence.

One of the most important issues addressed by Mohawk leadership in the last 50 years is the Indians' need and right to own more of their ancestral land. During the 1950s, the governments of Canada and the United States entered into an agreement to construct the St. Lawrence Seaway, a series of locks, dams, and canals along the river that would connect the Atlantic Ocean and the Great Lakes. Since Akwesasne and Kahnawake are located on the shores of the St. Lawrence, this project affected them immediately. The St. Lawrence Seaway Act of 1955 allocated funds for the seaway's construction and granted federal governments the right to expropriate land in the project's path. Tracts amounting to 1,260 acres were expropriated at Kahnawake. The Seaway Authority offered monetary compensation, but the band council and many residents refused to surrender their lands.

When the land was taken without their consent, the Kahnawake Mohawk appealed to the United Nations in 1959, claiming that their human rights, pro-tected by the UN Charter, had been violated. Chief Matthew Lazare petitioned the secretary-general and the Human Rights Commission:

> In violation of treaties between the Six Nations and Britain, and in contradiction to principles of international law, the Canadian authorities have deprived, and continue to deprive, our people of their inherent rights of possession of their land and property by confiscating real and personal property without due process of law and without just, adequate and prompt compensation, in connection with the opening of the St. Lawrence Seaway and other public projects. The method of confiscation is accomplished by brutal force which is unnecessary and unreasonable.

Chief Lazare pointed out that the amount of compensation offered to Indians at Kahnawake and Akwesasne was lower than that extended to non-Indian owners of land along the seaway. Lazare and others hoped that the United Nations would exert pressure on Canada to

> reverse its policy of depriving our sacred Reserve which is the only thing of value left to us, and to refrain from further encroachment on our land and infringement of our rights.

Although UN delegates expressed their sympathy to the Kahnawake Council,

MOHAWK POPULATION, 1991

	Resident	Nonresident	Total
Kahnawake	5,591	287	5,878
Kanesatake	760	474	1,234
Tyendinega	1,753	3,084	4,837
Gibson	120	340	460
Six Nations	7,723	7,669	15,392*
Akwesasne:			
Ontario	4,775	1,899	6,674
Quebec	3,395	185	3,580
New York	1,978	290	2,268
TOTALS	26,095	14,228	40,323

*This figure represents the entire population at Six Nations. There are 7,017 Mohawk members enrolled at the reserve.

they took no action to solve the Indians' problem.

In Akwesasne, the St. Lawrence Seaway expropriated 88 acres at Raquette Point, a piece of land on the American side of the reserve that juts out into the St. Lawrence River. The land was removed in order to straighten out the river channel. The Seaway Authority promised a payment of $100,000, only $31,000 of which has yet been paid. In addition, the authority took Barnhardt Island in the St. Lawrence to build a huge dam. The 3-member Akwesasne Council on the American side sued for $34 million in compensation. The New York courts rejected the suit, and in 1959 the U.S. Supreme Court similarly denied their claim. Despite these decisions, the Akwesasne Mohawk have pursued the case. Negotiations are currently under way for a just settlement for Barnhardt Island.

On the Canadian side of Akwesasne, the Seaway Authority expropriated land at Cornwall Island to build an international bridge between Ontario and New York. It expropriated additional acreage there for a Canadian customs station and tollbooths. The customs station and toll collection raised important issues concerning treaty rights. According to Jay's Treaty, a 1794 agreement between Great Britain and the United States, Indians at Akwesasne have the right to cross the border whenever they wish. The Seaway Authority ignored these basic rights by compelling the Akwesasne Mohawk to undergo customs inspections and pay tolls at the international bridge.

After many years of attempting a peaceful mediation of the dispute, the Akwesasne Mohawk blockaded the bridge during the winter of 1969. Only after this action did Canadian authorities finally take notice of the Indians' complaints. They responded by issuing bridge passes to Indians living on the Canadian side of Akwesasne but denied them to those on the American side. The policies enforcing customs inspections were not altered until the 1980s. Now the Akwesasne Mohawk are at last able to exercise the right of free passage that had been guaranteed to them by George Washington and King George III.

Other disputes over land arose at Akwesasne in the 1970s. Akwesasne residents, led by hereditary chiefs and members of the Longhouse Religion, claimed rights to two islands in the St. Lawrence River in 1970. After a group of Mohawk had occupied the islands for several months, Canadian authorities legally recognized the Akwesasne residents as the owners of the islands.

Three years later, another group of Mohawk, mostly from Akwesasne and Kahnawake, moved onto an unoccupied children's camp at Moss Lake in the Adirondack Mountains of New

Two Mohawk men guarding the entrance to Ganienkeh. In 1974, the Mohawk took over the area, claiming that this portion of their traditional territory had been illegally seized by New York State.

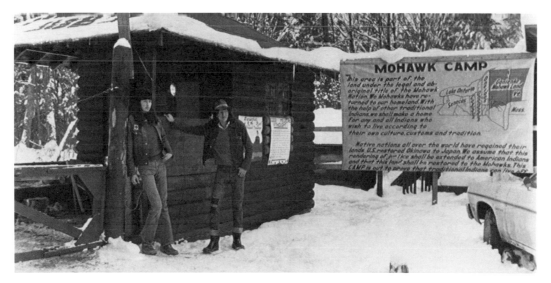

York. The land was in an area claimed by the Mohawk as part of their original territory that never had been legally sold to New York. After occupying the camp for three years, the Mohawk agreed to exchange this site for state land in nearby Clinton County. They named their new community Ganien-keh (ga-NYEN-ge), meaning "at the flint," and have tried to reestablish many aspects of traditional Mohawk culture there.

In 1970, the New York State Sub-committee on Indian Affairs began an investigation into conditions on Indian reservations, including Akwesasne. Committee members traveled to the reservations and heard testimony from Indian leaders. The panel documented serious problems in education, health, and housing. They recommended more local involvement in planning and staffing programs, more input into developing school curricula reflecting Indian languages and culture, and more funding for housing and health care.

Akwesasne residents have since taken advantage of federal funding available to them to promote bilingual and bicultural education. Several groups have published dictionaries, grammar books, and readers created to help teach children the Mohawk language. Books that recount Mohawk folklore and explain traditional crafts have also been prepared for use at schools attended by Akwesasne children. Most children residing on the American side attend schools in nearby towns; on the Canadian side, however, youngsters are educated at three elementary schools on the reserve. Older students commute to the Canadian city of Cornwall, just across the St. Lawrence River from Cornwall Island.

One Akwesasne leader, Ernest Benedict, founded an innovative educational and cultural program in the 1960s called the North American Indian Travelling College (NAITC). Benedict and other activists traveled to reserves throughout Canada to encourage Indian children's awareness of their cultural heritage and help them maintain their traditions. Since the mid-1970s, the NAITC has established a permanent location on Cornwall Island at Akwesasne and greatly expanded its resources. Currently headed by Barbara Barnes, the NAITC includes a cultural center, library, and museum.

At Six Nations, several organizations encourage learning the traditional languages and cultures of the people. The Woodlands Cultural Centre in Brantford, Ontario, sponsors numerous projects to develop teaching materials and publish books for children and adults.

The health of the people and of the land is another critical problem. At Akwesasne, many farmers noticed damage to their land and animals that they suspected was due to pollution from a nearby Reynolds Aluminum plant. After extensive health surveys by private and public organizations, Reynolds agreed in 1989 to pay $625,000 in

Akwesasne Mohawk students are taught about their tribe's language and traditions in local schools.

compensation to Akwesasne farmers. The General Motors Corporation has also undertaken a cleanup of a toxic dump at their plant near the reservation.

A fundamental issue of concern to the Mohawk in New York and Canada is that of sovereignty—the right to govern one's own nation and control one's destiny. Most leaders strongly believe that Mohawk sovereignty is guaranteed by numerous treaties signed with the United States and Canada. In accordance with these beliefs, leaders of Akwesasne conveyed their thoughts to New York State officials in 1970:

> We are not citizens of state or nation; we have our own nation—the Six Nations. You have no right to legislate for us nor we for you.
> We are frequently reminded that New York gives us many things. Let

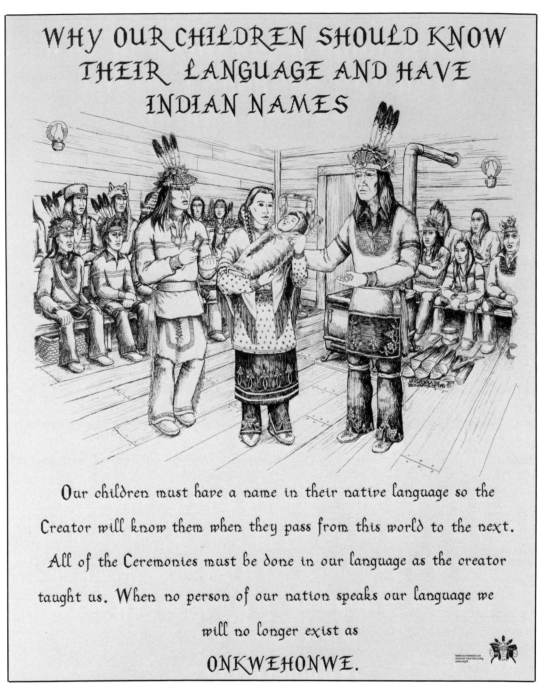

WHY OUR CHILDREN SHOULD KNOW THEIR LANGUAGE AND HAVE INDIAN NAMES

Our children must have a name in their native language so the Creator will know them when they pass from this world to the next. All of the Ceremonies must be done in our language as the creator taught us. When no person of our nation speaks our language we will no longer exist as

ONKWEHONWE.

The North American Indian Travelling College at Akwesasne prepares a variety of educational material to encourage Mohawk children to learn about their heritage. This poster explains the importance of studying the Mohawk language.

us remind you—many Indians work as ironworkers, factory workers, tradesmen. We pay income taxes and gas taxes.

St. Regis reservation was once much larger. Restore it. If we must go through courts you have lost the opportunity to be honorable.

The Mohawk are all one nation, even if some are in Canada.

Both New York State and U.S. federal authorities have been unwilling to grant recognition of total Indian sovereignty and yet have not denied its legitimacy. In one important development on the sovereignty issue, Quebec officials in 1984 signed an agreement with the Kahnawake Council to construct a hospital on the reserve. The wording of this document suggested that the agreement had been made between two legitimate governments. It marked the first time the Canadian government had, in effect, recognized the government of an Indian band as its equal.

New disputes over land and sovereignty continue to arise, however. In the summer of 1990, Oka, a town adjacent to Kanesatake, announced plans to expand a golf course into a wooded area that the town maintained it owned. The Mohawk at Kanesatake claimed that this land belonged to their reserve. In an attempt to stop construction of the golf course, a group from Kanesatake blockaded a road leading to the contested area. Quebec provincial authorities responded by sending po-

lice and army troops to confront the protesters. After weeks of negotiations, the Canadian government proposed to pay Oka for the land and transfer it to Kanesatake. Most of the Mohawk agreed to the settlement, and the blockade was lifted. However, some people occupied a community building at Kanesatake for more than two months to bring public attention to the plight of Indian peoples in Canada. When the people finally left the building, they were arrested and charged with rioting.

Indian groups throughout Canada responded to the conflict at Kanesatake by erecting blockades on their own reserves to show their support of the Mohawk. In British Columbia and Alberta, protestors stopped transportation along several railroad lines. And at Kahnawake, a Mohawk group blockaded the Mercier Bridge that connects Montreal and the southern shore of the St. Lawrence near the reserve.

Another recent controversy at Akwesasne involved the growth of casino gambling on the reserve. The problem began in the 1980s when several Akwesasne residents opened casinos. The traditional Council of Chiefs has steadfastly opposed casinos, which they see as disruptive to their traditional way of life. The elected tribal trustees, however, support residents' rights to operate these establishments.

After simmering for many years, the debate finally erupted during the spring and summer of 1990, when both opponents and supporters erected blockades at several casinos and roads. Troopers from New York State and police from Canada occupied Akwesasne for several weeks in July 1990. Although state and provincial police departed soon afterward, tensions decreased only slightly.

The Mohawk Council of Chiefs, supported by the Iroquois Confederacy, appealed to the U.S. government for help. They argued that, according to Jay's Treaty, the federal authorities had an obligation to protect Akwesasne against danger from outside influences.

They claimed that because casino gambling was originally a practice of non-Indians, they had a responsibility to prohibit it within reservation boundaries. Other Mohawk still assert that residents have a right to operate these businesses regardless of state or federal regulations. Government officials have not supported either position.

Disagreements among the Mohawk will undoubtedly continue. However, efforts are under way to develop new ways to mediate problems and achieve compromises. In October 1990, a com-

The members of the 1978 lacrosse team of the Akwesasne Reserve. Playing lacrosse—a sport originated by North American Indians—is one of the ways the Mohawk of today keep their traditions alive.

mittee of the New York State Assembly issued a statement calling into question the state's imposition of an elective system of government at Akwesasne in the 19th century. It recommended that this system be abolished and replaced with whatever form of government the community chooses.

Much has changed for the Iroquois over the centuries. Most likely, Mohawk people at Akwesasne, Kahnawake, Kanesatake, Six Nations, and Tyendinega will probably not be able to create a government based wholly on the principles of the ancient Confederacy—to be of One Heart, One Mind, One Law. However, they are committed to protect their sovereignty, secure their rights, and live in the ways that best suit their aspirations. Knowledge of their history and satisfaction with their past and present achievements will no doubt keep alive their pride in being the People of the Place of Flint, the respected Keepers of the Eastern Door. ▲

BIBLIOGRAPHY

Colden, Cadwallader. *The History of the Five Indian Nations.* 1727. Reprint. Ithaca: Cornell University Press, 1958.

Ghobashy, Omar. *The Caughnawaga Indians and the St. Lawrence Seaway.* New York: Devin-Adair, 1961.

Hertzberg, Hazel. *The Great Tree and the Longhouse.* New York: Macmillan, 1966.

Morgan, Lewis. *League of the Iroquois.* 1851. Reprint. New York: Corinth Books, 1962.

Tehanetorens. *Tales of the Iroquois.* Rooseveltown, NY: Akwesasne Notes, 1976.

Trigger, Bruce, ed. *The Handbook of North American Indians.* Vol. 15, *The Northeast.* Washington, DC: Smithsonian Institution, 1978.

Wilson, Edmund, and Joseph Mitchell. *Apologies to the Iroquois: With a Study of the Mohawks in High Street.* New York: Vintage Books, 1959.

THE MOHAWK AT A GLANCE

TRIBE *Mohawk*

CULTURE AREA *Northeast*

GEOGRAPHY *Eastern New York State and western New England; Mohawk and Hudson River valleys*

LINGUISTIC FAMILY *Iroquoian*

CURRENT POPULATION *Approximately 32,000*

FEDERAL STATUS *Native bands in Canada: Akwesasne, Kahnawake, Kanesatake, Tyendinega, Six Nations; tribal reservation in New York: Akwesasne*

GLOSSARY

agent A person appointed by the Bureau of Indian Affairs to supervise U.S. government programs on a reservation and/or in a specific region.

agriculture Intensive cultivation of tracts of land, sometimes using draft animals and heavy plowing equipment. Agriculture requires people to live in fairly permanent settlements.

Algonkians The Indian peoples living in the northeastern United States and east-central Canada whose languages are related and who share numerous cultural characteristics.

Algonquian The languages spoken by most Indian peoples in northeastern North America, including those who were geographically closest to the Iroquois.

allotment U.S. policy applied nationwide through the General Allotment Act of 1887, aimed at breaking up tribally owned reservations by assigning individual farms and ranches to Indians. Allotment was intended as much to discourage traditional communal activities as to encourage private farming and assimilate Indians into mainstream American life.

assimilation The complete absorption of one group into another group's cultural tradition.

Bureau of Indian Affairs (BIA) A U.S. government agency now within the Department of the Interior. Originally intended to manage trade and other relations with Indians, the BIA today seeks to develop and implement programs that encourage Indians to manage their own affairs and to improve their educational opportunities and general social and economic well-being.

clan A multigenerational group having a shared identity, organization, and property based on belief in their descent from a common ancestor. Because clan members consider themselves closely related, marriage within a clan is strictly prohibited.

confederacy A union of related tribes or nations that functions as a political, military, and/or economic unit.

culture The learned behavior of humans; nonbiological, socially taught activities; the way of life of a group of people.

fur trade Trading network in North America through which Indians gave Europeans animal pelts in exchange for manufactured goods.

Handsome Lake Religion A religious movement (also known as the Longhouse Religion and the Good Word) founded in 1799 by a Seneca man named Handsome Lake. This faith encouraged a return to traditional Iroquoian ways.

Iroquoian A large group of separate tribal peoples in the Northeast and Carolina regions speaking related languages and having similar cultures. Most were eventually conquered or incorporated by the Six Nations. Also, the languages spoken by these tribal groups.

Iroquois The members of a confederacy of Iroquoian peoples. Founded in about 1500, the Iroquois Confederacy originally included the Mohawk, Oneida, Onondaga, Cayuga, and Seneca. The Tuscarora joined the Iroquois League in 1722.

Jesuit A member of the Society of Jesus, a Roman Catholic order founded by Saint Ignatius of Loyola in 1534. The Jesuits are highly learned and, in the 17th century, were particularly active in spreading Christianity outside Europe.

lineage A group of individuals related through descent from a common ancestor; a descent group whose members recognize as relatives people on the mother's side only or the father's side only.

longhouse A structure with a frame made of cedar covered with bark and branches in which most Iroquoian peoples, including the Mohawk, lived. These dwellings were up to 200 feet long and could house 10 or 12 families.

matrilineal descent Rules for determining family or clan membership by tracing kinship through female ancestors.

mission A religious center founded by advocates of a particular denomination who are trying to convert nonbelievers to their faith.

missionaries Advocates of a particular religion who travel to convert nonbelievers to their faith.

moiety A grouping of clans. The Mohawk Nation was divided into two moieties.

nation A term used generally by the early Europeans in North America to describe the Indian tribal societies they encountered. Broadly, any large group of people having similar institutions, language, customs, and political and social ties.

removal policy A federal policy of the early 19th century that called for the sale of all Indian land in the eastern United States and the migration of Indians from these areas to lands west of the Mississippi River.

reservation, reserve A tract of land retained by Indians foir their own occupation and use. *Reservation* is used to describe such lands in the United States; *reserve,* in Canada.

treaty A contract negotiated between representatives of the U.S. government or another national government and one or more Indian tribes. Treaties dealt with the cessation of military action, the surrender of political independence, the establishment of boundaries, terms of land sales, and related matters.

tribe A society consisting of several or many separate communities united by kinship, culture, language, and other social institutions including clans, religious organizations, and warrior societies.

wampum Shell beads used by tribes in the northeastern United States in strings or belts as a pledge of the truth of their words, symbols of high office, records of diplomatic negotiations and treaties, and records of other important events.

ACKNOWLEDGMENTS

I wish to thank Mr. Ernest Benedict of Akwesasne for his generous aid in reading a draft of this book. His helpful suggestions were most welcome and appreciated. I would also like to acknowledge, with gratitude, Ms. Gloria Thompson for her kind hospitality throughout the years. I also want to thank Ms. Beatrice Francis for teaching me about the Mohawk language. Finally, thanks to all the people of Akwesasne, from whom I have learned so much.

PICTURE CREDITS

NANCY BONVILLAIN is associate professor of anthropology at the State University of New York at Stony Brook and an adjunct professor at the Graduate Faculty, New School for Social Research. She has a Ph.D. in anthropology from Columbia University. Dr. Bonvillain has written a grammar and dictionary of the Mohawk language and *The Huron* (1989) and has edited *Studies in Iroquois Culture* (1980). She has received grants from the National Endowment for the Humanities, the National Museum of Canada, and the American Philosophical Society for her research in 17th- and 18th-century Iroquoian history.

FRANK W. PORTER III, general editor of INDIANS OF NORTH AMERICA, is director of the Chelsea House Foundation for American Indian Studies. He holds a B.A., M.A., and Ph.D. from the University of Maryland. He has done extensive research concerning the Indians of Maryland and Delaware and is the author of numerous articles on their history, archaeology, geography, and ethnography. He was formerly director of the Maryland Commission on Indian Affairs and American Indian Research and Resource Institute, Gettysburg, Pennsylvania, and he has received grants from the Delaware Humanities Forum, the Maryland Committee for the Humanities, the Ford Foundation, and the National Endowment for the Humanities, among others. Dr. Porter is the author of *The Bureau of Indian Affairs* in the Chelsea House KNOW YOUR GOVERNMENT series.